W9-CPG-208

Anatomy of Interrogation Themes

THE REID TECHNIQUE OF INTERVIEWING AND INTERROGATION

Louis C. Senese
Vice President
John E. Reid and Associates
Chicago, Illinois

© 2005 Copyright John E. Reid and Associates, Inc. and Louis C. Senese

Library of Congress Control Number: 2005920943
ISBN 0-9760093-1-5

Published by John E. Reid and Associates, Inc.
209 West Jackson Blvd., 4th Floor, Chicago, IL 60606
www.Reid.com
Designed and printed by Hahn Printing Incorporated
752 North Adams Road, Eagle River, Wisconsin 54521

First Edition, Second Printing

TABLE OF CONTENTS

Anatomy of Interrogation Themes
THE REID TECHNIQUE OF INTERVIEWING AND INTERROGATION

ABOUT THE AUTHOR

After receiving his Bachelor of Science degree in Business Administration from Northern Illinois University, Louis C. Senese began training at John E. Reid and Associates, Inc. in 1972. In 1973 he became a state licensed polygraph examiner in Illinois and two years later received his Masters of Science degree in Detection of Deception from Reid College. After eight years as a staff polygraph examiner, he was promoted to Chief Polygraph Examiner and vice-president of the firm. He was responsible for overseeing seven to eight thousand interviews and interrogations for each of the next eight years. During this period he was responsible for quality control of the staff in addition to supervising students being trained in the polygraph technique. Louis has personally conducted in excess of eight thousand interviews and interrogations and has testified in Federal and State courts as well as employment hearings. He is a member of the Special Agents Association, the American Society of Industrial Security, the American Polygraph Association and past president of the Illinois Polygraph Society.

Mr. Senese later became involved in the seminar division of the firm and has conducted hundreds of training seminars on the Reid Technique of Interviewing and Interrogation® as well as specialized training programs throughout the United States and also in Belgium, Bosnia-Herzegovina, Canada, the Czech Republic, Germany, Japan, Mexico, the Netherlands, Puerto Rico, Saudi Arabia, Singapore and South Korea.

NOTICE

This book contains materials relating to interviewing and interrogation techniques developed and used by John E. Reid and Associates, Inc. in teaching a course on Criminal Interrogation and Behavior Analysis Interviews to law enforcement officers and others involved in security investigations. The course is taught under the name of The Reid Technique of Interviewing and Interrogation.

A description of this process, as taught in such courses, has been included herein with the consent of John E. Reid and Associates, Inc. and may be used by the reader in his or her work as an investigator. However, John E. Reid and Associates has retained all property rights to teaching such material in its course and others may use no part of these techniques for commercial purposes in teaching similar courses without written consent from John E. Reid and Associates, Inc.

The interrogation themes presented in this book are intended to serve as a guide for the investigator. Certainly, additional themes may be developed for each specific crime and each unique situation.

This book was written on the presumption that the reader has a good understanding of The Reid Technique®, either by having attended one of our training programs or by reading our books: Criminal Interrogations and Confessions, Inbau, Reid, Buckley and Jayne, 4th edition, 2002; The Investigator Anthology, Jayne and Buckley, 2000; or Essentials of The Reid Technique: Criminal Interrogation and Confessions *(Abridged)*, 2005, Inbau, Reid, Buckley and Jayne. If the reader does not have a solid foundation in The Reid Technique, some of the material in this book may not be understood in the proper context. In fact, some of the information contained herein could easily be misunderstood, misconstrued or used in an inappropriate manner by individuals who have not been Reid trained in or possess a basic understanding of the Reid Technique.

Due to the special nature of this book, with its discourse between interrogator and suspect, the words "he" and "him" are used generically to include both male and female persons. In addition the words "guilty," "deceptive," "innocent" and "truthful" represent nothing more than labels to identify the status of the person under discussion. Obviously, a person's guilt or innocence can only be determined through a criminal trial.

DEDICATION

John E. Reid (1910-1982) gave me the opportunity to begin my training in polygraph at John E. Reid and Associates in 1972. I am most grateful to Mr. Reid for sharing his skills and passion in polygraph and the art of interviewing and interrogation. The past thirty plus years of practicing these skills have been indescribably rewarding.

Successfully identifying and obtaining a legally acceptable confession from the offender has been the true fulfillment of this profession. Knowing the offender's conviction will in some way be a moral victory for the victim and potential future victims is even more gratifying. Additionally, as I have become more involved in the instruction of this technique, knowing that others will be acting in such a positive manner to identify offenders is likewise very rewarding.

This text could not have been written had it not been for the contributions, dedication and commitment to the Reid Technique by the following staff: Joseph P. Buckley, Daniel S. Malloy, William P. Schrieber, James J. Bobal, Mark D. Reid, David M. Buckley, Brian Jayne, Michael J. Adamec, Arthur T. Newey, Michael F. Masokas and Rick Sjoberg.

I would especially like to thank my colleague, Daniel S. Malloy for providing many ideas and examples for this book, but more importantly for being a great training partner and a most valued friend. I am also grateful to Joseph P. Buckley, President of John E. Reid and Associates, not only for his continued support in writing this book but also for generously agreeing to read the entire manuscript and offering extremely insightful suggestions.

INTRODUCTION

Today I was driving to report for jury duty at the 18th Judicial Circuit Court located in DuPage County, Illinois. Never having served on jury duty before, I was looking forward to the opportunity to vindicate the truthful or find the violator guilty. I figure it this way; people need to be accountable for their behavior when they violate the law. I was advised to report by 9:00 a.m. After driving my daughter to school, I found myself running a little late. On my way to jury duty I noticed the speed limit to be 40 mph.

I consider myself to be a very good driver since I haven't received a traffic citation for over 15 years. I haven't been in a traffic accident since being a teenager. Plus, I'm driving a very safe car equipped with anti-lock brakes and front and side air bags. I always wear my seat belt. Furthermore, I regard myself as a reasonably intelligent person possessing very good common sense.

The time is getting closer to 9:00 a.m. and being that rush hour is over, there is not much traffic. I decide to increase my speed by 5 mph. The area I am driving in has no school zones and the day could not be better – bright, sunny, perfect visibility. Another car passes me, then another. The speed limit has not changed. I think back decades to my high school driver's education class and recall the instructor saying something to the effect that, "It's important for the driver to keep up with the flow of traffic." I accelerate another 5 mph. I am now going 50 mph in a 40 mph zone. I certainly don't want to be late to perform my civic duty and therefore increase the speed a little more. You see, I want to be sure to get there on time, be called for a case and be sure justice is served to those that violate the law.

What irony! Have I not justified speeding – breaking the law? How many ways have I rationalized my behavior? I'm sure you can find several examples in the above account of how I justified my illegal behavior as reasonable. Have you ever rationalized or justified your own questionable behavior?

That same justification process is developed in the mind of the criminal offender. Most offenders recognize that they are violating the law when they commit a crime. In fact, they go to great lengths to conceal their behavior so as to avoid the consequences associated with the detection of their criminal behavior. Whenever illegal or unethical behavior is chosen, there is a corresponding fear of consequence associated with the discovery of that behavior. Primarily, one's fear of consequence can range from jail (or loss of freedom), loss of job (or security), to loss of social standing, restitution and embarrassment. Consequently, in order to live with their behavior and the belief that they are not such a *bad* person they rationalize or justify their behavior. First-time offenders learn to live with the anxiety or internal conflict created by denying their behavior. Interestingly, as a crime is repeated without being detected, a fascinating psychological phenomenon occurs. The suspect's anxiety and conflict associated with lying or concealing the crime begins to diminish due to the positive rewards associated with the negative behavior of the crime, e.g., profiting from the sale of drugs or the sale of classified or proprietary information; dominance and control in a rape; discipline in a child abuse situation; ego gratification as a result of creating a computer virus; etc. In fact, the crime can eventually become a "normal" way of life for the offender. Examples of this behavior have unfortunately been seen in gang members, pedophiles, embezzlers, drug dealers, and the likes of Ted Bunde, John Gacy, and Jeffrey Dahmer, to name just a few.

This book will explore the various ways, via case examples and suspects' interview responses, just how we can logically determine in what ways the offender has justified his crime. We can therefore develop a strategy of how to present to the offender his own justifications and rationalizations in a morally, legally acceptable manner, with the primary goal of obtaining the truth – typically a full confession or admission of guilt. To further assist the reader, Chapter 6, Crimes and Related Themes, will detail a variety of crimes and offer various ways offenders have justified their criminal behavior. Hopefully, this information will provide a strategy for a majority of most criminal interrogations. *It is recommended that as the reader reviews the individual themes, he notes additional themes that can be used based on prior experience or ideas developed during the reading of this book.*

By the way, I never got called for jury duty. But rest assured, next time I do get called, I most certainly will leave earlier!

September 11, 2001, will remain a day that people all over the world will never forget. It was that most tragic day that became the impetus and defining moment for creating this text. We will always remember where we were and what we were doing during the morning hours of 9/11. Once the realization became evident of what had actually occurred on that day, I am sure that each and every American asked, "What can I do to help?"

Dan Malloy, my training partner was with me in Philadelphia conducting an interrogation seminar for a federal agency when we heard the horrifying news about the World Trade Center, the Pentagon and the plane crash in Pennsylvania. The seminar participants immediately made arrangements to report to their respective work locations. Both Dan and I reside in the Chicago area. Since all aircraft were grounded, we rented a car and without delay began our twelve-hour drive home. It was during this drive that we began to discover our answer to that most central question in everyone's mind, "How can I help?"

Since we have devoted our lives to interviewing and interrogation, we decided to develop specialized interrogation tactics (themes) addressing individuals suspected of terrorist activity. "The interrogation theme is the core of the Reid Nine Steps of Interrogation and is presented as a monologue in which reasons and excuses are offered to the suspect that will serve to psychologically, not legally, justify or minimize the moral seriousness of the specific illegal activity." These terrorist interrogation themes that were developed were subsequently mailed to many federal, state and local law enforcement agencies that we thought might find them to be beneficial. As a result of developing specific terrorist interrogation theme tactics, I began to realize that a compendium of interrogation themes addressing a variety of crimes would be a very useful resource for the investigator. That was the genesis of this book. The specific themes addressing terrorist activities, as well as others addressing a variety of crimes, are incorporated in Chapter 6. Hopefully this book will not only offer the investigator additional interrogation ideas, but will also inspire a thought process in which the investigator develops additional theme tactics of his own.

The irony in the timing of the publication of this book was that I was training United States military investigators/interrogators with my partner Dan Malloy at two separate government military facilities in South Korea, when we heard about the shocking pre-interrogation procedures and abuses that occurred at the Abu Ghraib prison site in Iraq. Subsequently, Secretary of Defense Donald Rumsfeld and General Richard Meyers, Chairman of the Joint Chiefs of Staff, visited this site at which time Defense Secretary Rumsfeld stated that the abuses of the Iraqi detainees were a "body blow for all of us. It doesn't represent America and it doesn't represent American values." Those words validate our philosophy of interrogation in that for quite some time our company has been teaching the U. S. military a non-violent empathetic and sympathetic approach toward the interrogation of suspects, namely the

Reid Technique.

In fact, this author and his training partner, Dan Malloy, at the end of March of 2004, were also in Prague, in the Czech Republic, training military intelligence organizations on The Reid Technique of Interviewing and Interrogation. These are just two of the many instances where we had the privilege and opportunity to instruct government investigators and interrogators on the Reid Technique of Interviewing and Interrogation. It is the opinion of our firm that the incidents at the Abu Ghraib prison in Iraq were an aberration and contradiction to the United States of America's position with respect to interviewing and interrogation tactics and techniques of criminal suspects and prisoners. It is also a core principle of the Reid Technique and, in particular theme development, to treat all suspects under interrogation with dignity and respect, and in a way everyone would and should expect to be treated.

"And ye shall know the truth, and the truth shall make you free."

John 8:32

Chapter 1

The Genesis of the Reid Technique

John E. Reid (August 16, 1910-January 11, 1982) was a former Chicago Police Officer. He received his law degree from DePaul University and subsequently founded John E. Reid and Associates, a private polygraph practice.

He joined the Chicago Police Department in 1936 as a patrol officer. In 1940, he accepted a position in the Chicago Police Scientific Crime Detection Laboratory, where he was trained as a polygraph examiner and interrogator under the direction of Fred Inbau (1909-1998), who was the first lab director. Mr. Inbau went on to become a professor of law at Northwestern University Law School and retired from the school as a John Henry Wigmore Professor of Law. Professor Inbau was the founder of Americans for Effective Law Enforcement, AELE (1966). The two became lifelong friends, contributing greatly to the field of polygraph and the art of interviewing and interrogation. In 1947, Reid left the Chicago Police Department to form his own company, John E. Reid and Associates, Inc.

While in private practice, Mr. Reid began developing various questions that he would ask suspects during the interview preceding a polygraph examination. He observed similar verbal and nonverbal responses to the same specific questions from truthful suspects and likewise, similar verbal and nonverbal responses from the deceptive suspects to the same questions. This was the beginning of the Reid Behavior Analysis Interview. This interview has become a standard questioning technique in determining an individual's truthfulness to the issue under investigation.

Fred Inbau's expertise was in the development of interrogation strategies. John Reid worked with Fred Inbau in refining the interrogation process and eventually developed it into the current technique that is referred to as "The Reid Nine Steps of Interrogation."

The Reid Nine Steps of Interrogation and the Behavior Analysis Interview became integral parts of the training program called "The Reid Technique of Interviewing and Interrogation." This training program was first presented to outside investigators in 1974. Since that time this seminar has been presented by John E. Reid and Associates throughout the world. Currently the firm conducts in excess of 300 such programs annually.

Chapter 2

Overview of the Reid Behavior Analysis Interview

This chapter is intended to act as a review of the Reid Behavior Analysis Interview (BAI) for investigators that have either attended our seminar program or for those that have read one of our texts, <u>Criminal Interrogation and Confessions</u> or the <u>Essentials of The Reid Technique: Criminal Interrogation and Confessions</u> (*Abridged*). John E. Reid and his colleagues developed over the years a structured set of "behavior-provoking questions" to include in the interview process, along with the traditional investigative questions of who, what, where, when, how and why.   Each of these specific behavior-provoking questions has a fundamental principle that discriminates between truthful and deceptive responses. However, no one question or answer is determinative. The investigator must consider the totality of the suspect's verbal and nonverbal responses as well as all of the available case facts and evidence before rendering an opinion as to the suspect's truth or deception.

During the interview process an effort should be made to establish rapport with the suspect, as well as a behavioral baseline. Engaging in casual conversation and asking non-threatening questions about the suspect's name, address, place of employment, job responsibilities, etc. can oftentimes establish this rapport and behavioral baseline.

The following will provide a review of the behavior-provoking questions, the principle of response for each question and conclude with examples of typical truthful and deceptive answers.   This BAI will focus on a hypothetical internal theft of $10,000 from a company. It is assumed that the employees have been given prior notification of the interviews. The employees are also aware that everyone working in the section where the money is missing will be questioned.

1. (Reason) "Do you know the reason for your interview today?"
    (Principle) Truthful feel comfortable discussing the issue and many times use realistic words in their answer.
    (Truthful) "Sure, it's about the $10,000 that was stolen."
    (Deceptive) "Not really, I guess something happened."

2. (History/You) "We are investigating the missing $10,000. Did you steal that $10,000?"
    (Principle) Truthful offer an immediate, direct denial. Deceptive many times will not answer the question verbally; respond with a question; use non-contracted denials; or will hesitate before the denial.
    (Truthful) "No, absolutely not." Or, "No, I didn't."
    (Deceptive) "Why would I take the money?" "You're assuming the money was actually stolen, aren't you?" Or, "No, I did not."

3. (Knowledge) "Do you know for sure who stole the missing $10,000?"
    (Principle) Truthful may offer a name or if not, display sincere regret for not being able to help the investigator. Deceptive offer a denial without any serious thought, respond with a non-contracted denial or lack general concern.
    (Truthful) "I think there is one person that had the need and

opportunity to take the money."

(Deceptive) "No, I do not." Or, "How would I know?"

4. (Suspicion) "Who do you think did take the missing $10,000? Understand that I am not asking you if you know for sure who took the money. I am asking what individuals you simply have a gut feeling for who may have taken the money."

(Principle) Truthful show sincere interest and may offer names and respond with reasonable explanations for their answer when asked to explain. Deceptive may suggest individuals, but lack sincerity for their suspicion. Deceptive may also respond with a very broad answer.

(Truthful) "Well, there are two people that come to mind. This one guy Dan does have a gambling problem and Mike is very disgruntled."

(Deceptive) "I suspect no one." Or, "I think anyone could have taken the money."

5. (Vouch) "Is there anyone that you feel you can vouch for and say you do not think would have taken the $10,000?"

(Principle) The truthful suspect feels comfortable vouching for individuals, eliminating them from suspicion. The deceptive may vouch for himself alone and is less likely to vouch for others. Their intent is to keep the focus of the investigation as broad as possible.

(Truthful) "There are two or three people that I don't think took the money. I don't think Joe took it because he wasn't even working the day it was stolen. Mary and I go way back and I know that she is very honest. Dave is responsible for the money and I don't think he'd take money because he'd be the first person that the company would look at."

(Deceptive) "I would vouch for everyone." Or, "I can only vouch for myself." Or, "I don't know the people that well so I guess I couldn't vouch for anyone."

6. (Attitude) "How do you feel about being interviewed concerning the missing $10,000?"
   (Principle) The truthful will usually accept and understand the purpose of the interview. The deceptive often will become defensive, argumentative or negative. Deceptive are more likely than the truthful to use the word "scared" in their response.
   (Truthful) "It's okay, I understand that you have to investigate the loss; after all, $10,000 is a lot of money."
   (Deceptive) "I don't like it one bit. I don't like being accused." Or, "It's kind of scary."

7. (Credibility) "Do you think that the $10,000 was actually stolen?"
   (Principle) The truthful will usually acknowledge the credibility of the offense. The deceptive are less likely to suggest the crime occurred – it is their intent to have the investigator think another factor caused the loss; in this case, perhaps negligence.
   (Truthful) "Yeah, I think the money was stolen! It just didn't get up and walk away."
   (Deceptive) "That's a good question. Maybe it was misplaced. I'm sure it will turn up sooner or later."

7a. (Credibility) If the suspect has been accused by someone of committing the crime this question would be asked. "When Mike says that he saw you take the missing $10,000, is he lying?"
    (Principle) Truthful individuals will confidently state that the accuser is lying.
    (Truthful) "Absolutely he's lying; I never stole a penny from the company."

(Deceptive) "I'm not saying he's lying; maybe he's mistaken." Or, "I know what I did."

8. (Opportunity) "Who do you think would have had the best opportunity to take the money? I'm not saying he did, but who would have had the best chance or opportunity?"
    (Principle) Truthful suspects are willing to indicate the opportunity if appropriate. The deceptive may expand the investigation by naming unrealistic suspects.
    (Truthful) "Myself, Kristen and Genna, we all handled the money."
    (Deceptive) "I guess almost anyone could have done it."

9. (Motive) "Why do you think someone stole the missing $10,000?"
    (Principle) Truthful suspects feel comfortable discussing motives. The deceptive feel uncomfortable because they would be revealing why they stole the money.
    (Truthful) " I think they really needed the money or are just dishonest."
    (Deceptive) "How would I know?" Or, "I really haven't thought about it."

10. (Think) "Did you just think about taking this $10,000?"
    (Principle) The more serious the offense, the more reliable this question is but generally, truthful suspects reject the suggestion of thinking about committing the crime. Because the deceptive has committed the crime, he has already thought about it and in fact believes that anyone else in his situation would have done the same. The deceptive many times qualify their answer.
    (Truthful) "No way." Or, "Not at all."
    (Deceptive) "You always think about it." Or, "Not seriously."

11. (Objection) "Tell me why you wouldn't take that $10,000?"
    (Principle) The truthful tend to answer in the first person.
    (Truthful) "Because I'm not dishonest."
    (Deceptive) "Because it's against the law." Or, "It's against my religion."

12. (Punishment) "What do you think should happen to the person who took the missing $10,000?"
    (Principle) Truthful tend to suggest punishment appropriate for the crime and express a personal feeling. Deceptive tend to respond more leniently or avoid a personal opinion.
    (Truthful) "They should pay the money back and be prosecuted. What they did was no different than a common criminal."
    (Deceptive) "That's up to the company." Or, "I'm sure the company will terminate them."

13. (Investigative Results) "How do you think the results of the investigation will come out on you regarding the missing $10,000?" There is a variation of this question regarding the polygraph. It is recommended that the text, *Criminal Interrogations and Confessions* be referenced for proper explanation.
    (Principle) Truthful suspects usually indicate confidence that the results will exonerate them. The deceptive are more likely to qualify their answer with words such as "hope", "should", or "think." They are also less positive.
    (Truthful) "Fine, it will show I had nothing to do with it."
    (Deceptive) "I hope it clears me." Or, "I think it will show I didn't do it."

14. (Second Chance) "Do you think the person who stole the missing $10,000 deserves a second chance under any

circumstances?"

(Principle) Truthful suspects generally reject a second chance. The deceptive view this question as implying whether or not they should be given a second chance.

(Truthful) "No, once a thief always a thief."

(Deceptive) "If they are really sorry, sure." Or, "I believe so, if they had a good reason."

15. (Alibi/Account) "What was your relationship with the missing $10,000?"

(Principle) Truthful accounts contain appropriate details, give out of sequence information and may contain unnecessary information. The deceptive account is vague, provides sketchy details and is more likely to give a chronological account.

(Truthful) "The money was in the manager's office. I made the deposit a day earlier. I never was in the manager's office during the entire week that they say the money was stolen."

(Deceptive) "I believe I made the deposit at 3:00 p.m. I understand the money was in the manager's office. At 3:10 p.m. I took a fifteen-minute break and was reading the newspaper. I then went back to work at 3:25 p.m. I left work at 4:45."

16. (Tell Loved Ones) "Did you tell any of your family members about your interview today?"

(Principle) Truthful suspects are comfortable discussing the crime with their loved ones. Their loved ones will offer emotional support and generally not ask the suspect if he was involved in the crime.

(Truthful) "Sure, I told my wife/husband all about it."

(Deceptive) "No, I didn't want to worry her/him."

17. (Bait) "Is there any reason that if we reviewed the security film

that we would see you inside the manager's office on the day the money was stolen? I'm not suggesting that you stole the money but perhaps went in there for some other reason that you forgot about."

(Principle) Once the truthful provide their relationship with the crime they will not change their story. Since the deceptive is lying regarding his relationship with the crime, he may change his story when baited. Deceptive also are reluctant to answer this question. Truthful suspects usually spontaneously reject the implication of the bait.

(Truthful) "Absolutely not. If you review the tapes you will not see me going into the manager's office."

(Deceptive) "Now that I think about it, it is possible that I did go into the office after the deposit was made. But I only checked to see if the manager was there."

Chapter 3

Overview of the Reid Nine Steps of Interrogation

Following the Reid Behavior Analysis Interview (BAI), interrogation should only take place if the interrogator is reasonably certain of the suspect's deception to the issue under investigation. Typically, individuals believed to be deceptive to the issue under investigation are interrogated following their interview. The interrogation does not have to immediately follow the interview or even be conducted the same day, but generally would follow a suspect's interview.

John E. Reid and Associates developed the following Nine Steps of Interrogation through extensive practical experience obtained during hundreds of thousands of interrogations conducted for over half of a century. This section of the book is designed to provide the reader a brief overview of the Nine Steps of Interrogation. For a detailed description, it is highly recommended that the reader attend the seminar, The Reid Technique of Interviewing and Interrogation, or read the text, <u>Criminal Interrogation and Confessions</u>, 4th Edition, Inbau, et al or the <u>Essentials of The Reid Technique: Criminal Interrogations and Confessions</u> (*Abridged*). It is important that all interviews and interrogations meet all legal requirements, including the advisement of rights when necessary.

Ideally, the interrogation is conducted in a non-supportive (for the suspect) environment. The room should be free of distractions, preferably containing a desk and two chairs. The interrogator should not use the desk as a barrier, but should position the two chairs on the same side of the desk. If the suspect has a representative present during the interrogation such as an attorney, union representative, or parent, the seating arrangement should be modified. In this situation, the third party should be seated next to and slightly behind the suspect. The investigator remains seated facing the suspect.

Step 1: The Positive Confrontation

By accusing the suspect at the beginning of the interrogation, the interrogator immediately establishes an atmosphere of confidence and is also able to observe and evaluate the suspect's reaction to the accusation.

The interrogator enters the room while holding a case evidence file, stands approximately four or five feet directly in front of the suspect and unequivocally accuses the suspect of committing the crime. One note of caution at this early stage of the interrogation process: standing too close to the suspect might cause the suspect to retreat to a defensive posture (arms crossed, legs crossed, looking away, sitting sideways, etc.). This defensive posture may simply have been attributable to the interrogator's proxemics and orientation of being too close to the suspect at the beginning of the interrogation. This posture is indicative of a suspect who will offer greater resistance to telling the truth during the interrogation. If the interrogator had been standing four or five feet from the suspect at the beginning of Step 1, the suspect might not have retreated to a defensive posture based simply on the interrogator standing too close, but rather to a neutral or defeated posture (head and body slump, nodding head up and down in an affirmative action, etc.).

While standing in front of the suspect, the interrogator touches the case evidence file and begins with an innuendo of evidence, "In this file I have the results of our investigation regarding the missing $10,000." This statement is immediately followed with a direct accusation. "The results of our investigation clearly indicate that you took the missing $10,000."

When accusing the suspect, the interrogator should avoid using descriptive or emotionally charged phraseology that recreates the heinousness of the crime or reminds the suspect of the severe punishment associated with the act. In lieu of the word rape, the interrogator should use the phrase "forced to have intercourse"; instead of the term sexual harassment, the phrase might be, "inappropriately touched." In fact, a good guideline to follow when accusing suspects is to avoid the criminal statutes describing the crime and to substitute the offense with a word or phrase that unequivocally describes the crime but to a less graphic or in a less harsh manner.

The interrogator, still standing in front of the suspect pauses for three or four seconds to observe the suspect's reaction to the accusation. Nonverbally, the deceptive many times will break eye contact, slouch in the chair, cross legs, or turn sideways. Verbally, the deceptive many times will avoid denying the accusation. Challenging the interrogator generally increases the suspect's anxiety associated with lying. Instead of denying, many deceptive respond with a question, "Why would I take $10,000?" or offer no statement and just shake their heads.

After about four or five seconds of observing the suspect's response, the interrogator, still standing in front of the suspect begins his transition statement leading into Step 2, Theme Development. "As I said, there is no doubt that you did take the missing $10,000 but what I would like to do is to sit down with you and see if we can get this thing cleared up." The interrogator sits down, places the case evidence to the side, leans forward and begins to develop his themes. Step 1 takes approximately thirty seconds to accomplish.

Step 2: Theme Development

Most suspects have rationalized and justified their illegal behavior. The employee who steals may believe that he is being victimized, that his company generates huge profits, that he is being underpaid, he is being overworked – in essence, that he is being cheated and taken advantage of. Therefore, this employee has justified "taking" the money that the company should have paid him anyway. Likewise, the guy selling drugs in his neighborhood has justified his behavior by blaming his unemployment, blaming his responsibility to provide for his family, having a criminal record which makes it difficult to get a good job, not selling to young children, only selling to individuals approaching him and if he didn't provide the drug, someone else would.

As soon as the interrogator sits down in front of the suspect following the positive confrontation, he begins presenting reasons and excuses that will serve to psychologically (not legally) justify the suspect's behavior. Additionally, the interrogator minimizes the moral seriousness of the suspect's criminal behavior. Blame is shifted from the suspect to some other person or a set of circumstances that prompted him to commit the crime. For example, "I think you took that missing $10,000 because Joe didn't do his job and lock the money in the safe. Had Joe only locked the money in the safe as he was supposed to and not left the money out on the desk, you wouldn't be here. You know I'm right. This was obviously a spur-of-the-moment mistake on your part. I don't think you planned this thing, did you? Of course you didn't. If Joe only had done his job, we wouldn't be here right now, right?" Themes should be presented in a monologue format by the investigator.

It is highly recommended that the interrogator be prepared to present at least five reasons and excuses to the suspect as to why he committed the crime and at least five additional ways to minimize the suspect's criminal behavior. It is for this reason that I have presented dozens of crimes and hundreds of theme options in Chapter 6. During theme development, as the suspect listens to the interrogator, the suspect may reject many of the themes the interrogator offers. Once the interrogator presents the reason that the suspect relates most to, the interrogator might observe interest on the part of the suspect. This interest will generally result in eye contact, a nodding of the head, physical barriers opening, or no further denials. The investigator should then focus on that particular theme, eventually leading up to Step 7 in which an alternative question is used to develop the first admission of guilt.

The following is an example of theme development ideas for an individual selling crack-cocaine.

Themes which provide *reasons and excuses* that serve to psychologically, not legally justify the suspect's behavior include:

1. Intent was to support wife and daughter
2. No one would give you a decent-paying job
3. The buyers of the drugs approached you
4. The money was just too easy to pass up
5. This is basically supply and demand – if you didn't provide the drug, someone else would
6. Suggest the suspect was doing a favor for someone

Themes *minimizing* the moral seriousness of the suspect's criminal behavior include:
1. Contrast selling to adults versus children
2. Not selling inferior or dangerous drug, selling a good-quality

product

3. Suggest the suspect was only the provider of drugs, not the manufacturer or the head of a drug cartel
4. Not living the life of luxury, not driving a Mercedes, wearing designer clothes or living in a million dollar house, just getting by
5. No one was hurt, it was not like committing an armed robbery; in fact, there was no victim
6. Earning hundreds versus thousands of dollars per sale
7. Only selling for the last year or two versus the last ten years
8. Selling a stimulant versus PCP or some other deadly hallucinogenic drug or a date rape drug

"Frank, I know that you have had some dealings with the police before. I also know that you did some time (in jail). I also know you have to support a wife and daughter. If a guy has no job, no income and a family to provide for, sometimes a basically good person is forced to do something he normally would not do. That is exactly what I think happened to you. I think your family is the most important thing in your life and you would do just about anything to provide for them. If someone had offered you a decent job you would not be here now. People find it hard to forgive and forget mistakes people made in the past. Some people are just plain ignorant and they treat people that have make past mistakes like they're dirt; it's just not fair. Furthermore, these people that you were selling to, in all probability came to you, it's not like you went to their homes or places of work. If they didn't keep pestering you, maybe things would have been different. Plus the money was just too good to pass up. Maybe you could get a job making $6.00 to $7.00 an hour busting your butt earning you a pathetic $12,000 a year! I was reading somewhere that if you make under $13,000 a year you're considered living in poverty! How can you survive? You can't.

"Also Frank, you and I both know that if these people didn't come to you, they would go to someone else to get their supply. At least you are being fair in the price and selling a good-quality product. The way I look at it is if you were in a different country, maybe it would be legal! We can sell alcohol or cigarettes but not crack-cocaine. Why? Also Frank, it is my understanding that you are not selling to little kids but to consenting adults who have the ability to decide for themselves. I think that you are simply scratching out a living. I know you are not living in a million dollar house, driving a Mercedes and wearing designer clothes! But maybe you are not the guy I'm thinking you are. Maybe you do have so much money stashed away you could buy and sell anything. Is that the case? Do you have hundreds of thousands of dollars stashed away or are you living like most people, from hand to mouth? Have you made so much money selling crack that you can't even count that high or is it what I'm thinking, just enough to get by? Frank, are we talking about hundreds of thousands of dollars a week or just a few thousand? I'm thinking from talking to you that we're not talking hundreds of thousands of dollars, but I could be wrong. That is why I need to get this straight with you now. You haven't made hundreds of thousands of dollars, have you?"

It should be remembered that the interrogator's effort to develop a theme during the interrogation should focus on offering the suspect a moral excuse for his criminal behavior and never offer the suspect a promise of reduced punishment. It is critical to keep in mind that, "During the presentation of any theme based upon the morality factor, caution must be taken to avoid any indication that the minimization of the moral blame will relieve the suspect of criminal responsibility." (p. 235, Criminal Interrogation and Confessions, 4th edition). Furthermore, "the interrogator must avoid any expressed or specific statement that because of the minimized seriousness of the offense leniency will be afforded." (p. 246, Criminal Interrogation and Confessions, 4th edition).

Step 3: Denials

As the interrogator presents reasons and excuses to the suspect and attempts to minimize the moral seriousness of the suspect's behavior, denials should be anticipated. Most suspects will offer a denial following the positive confrontation. The strength of this denial should be evaluated to judge the strength of resistance that the suspect may offer during the interrogation. However, once the initial denial has been verbalized, the goal of the interrogator should be to attempt to discourage all subsequent denials during the theme development stage. The more the suspect denies his involvement, the more difficult it becomes for him to admit that he committed the crime.

Fortunately, there are certain telltale introductions that will alert the interrogator when a suspect is about to verbalize a denial. These include certain nonverbal indicators such as the suspect holding his hand up or shaking his head no or making eye contact. There are also verbal permission phrases that oftentimes accompany these nonverbal activities such as, "May I say one thing?" or "Could I say something?" If the interrogator allows the suspect to continue with his statement at this moment, almost certainly the suspect will deny his involvement in the commission of the crime.

Therefore, the interrogator should discourage the verbalization of the denials by interrupting the suspect with a command statement and referring to the suspect by name: " Jim, hold on for just a minute." Or, "Mary, let me just explain one thing first." As these statements are being made the interrogator can turn his head away and hold up his hand to suggest to the suspect that he should refrain from continuing his verbal statement.

The interrogator should then return to developing his themes.

Step 4: Objections

If the interrogator is successful in discouraging the suspect from verbalizing denials, the next step oftentimes involves an effort on the suspect's part to regain the offensive – to do this they may offer an objection. An objection is a statement proposed by the suspect that is an excuse or reason why the accusation against them is false. An example of a possible objection in the above-referred-to drug dealer interrogation would be the statement: "Why would I sell drugs; I have plenty of money in the bank?" Suspects view such statements as a way to establish their innocence; their thinking is that if I can prove I have a lot of money in the bank then it establishes the fact that I do not need to sell drugs because I already have enough money, therefore your accusation must be wrong. In fact, however, the objection statement does not prove that anything is wrong about the interrogator's conclusion that the suspect has been involved in selling drugs.

It is very important to recognize that most objections are usually true statements. The drug dealer probably does have money in the bank. The parent who abuses his child, denies the crime and presents the objection, "Why would I do such a terrible thing, I love my child?" probably does love his child. The government intelligence officer selling classified information to hostile countries responds, "Why would I do something like that; I have 20 years of dedicated service and I have Top Secret Clearance?" probably does have 20 years service and does have high-level clearance. In all of these examples of objections, not one of the statements was a direct denial to involvement in the offense. Generally speaking, only the deceptive individuals voice objections. When presented with an objection from the suspect the interrogator should use the objection as the very reason why the suspect should confess.

Since most objections are true statements, the proper manner in which to respond to an objection is to first agree with it and then talk about how it can be seen as a positive development for the suspect if the objection is true. The interrogator should respond to the objection as follows: "Frank, I'm glad you said that you have money in the bank. I'm sure you do. That tells me that you were probably doing favors for a few friends by getting them some cocaine, not doing it so much for the money. On the other hand, if you had no money in the bank, then that tells me that you are a major dealer, selling to anyone at anytime simply for the money."

If the interrogator had challenged the objection, telling the suspect it was not true, that he did not have money in the bank, the suspect would have continued interrupting and challenging the interrogator to view his bank accounts. If this had occurred, the focus of the interrogation would no longer be directed toward the development of the theme, but degenerate into a rather unsuccessful attempt to respond to the suspect's challenges that he did have money in the bank.

Step 5: Procurement and Retention of Suspect's Attention

Generally, at this step, the suspect is mentally withdrawing from the interrogation process by ignoring the interrogator's theme and focusing his thoughts on the various consequences of his crime. When this occurs, the suspect becomes quiet and establishes several physical barriers such as folding his arms across his chest, crossing one leg over the other, turning his body away from a direct frontal alignment with the interrogator or staring off to the side. At this point the suspect is content to allow the interrogator to continue to talk.

At this phase of the interrogation it is very important for the interrogator to gradually move physically closer to the suspect. The effect of the closer proxemics is to elevate the interrogator's credibility and to regain the suspect's attention onto what the interrogator is doing and saying. The interrogator should begin to focus the various theme concepts down to one or two essential elements that will eventually become the basis for the alternative question.

Step 6: Handling the Suspect's Passive Mood

This step is more of an observation of the suspect's behavior than a series of proactive steps for the interrogator to take. At this stage of the interrogation, the suspect is essentially psychologically resigned to tell the truth and generally recognizes the ineffectiveness of his previous attempts to convince the interrogator that he did not commit the crime. The suspect becomes less tense and more relaxed. The suspect may exhibit signs of this psychological resignation, such as moving into a head and body slump, taking deep breaths, beginning to nod the head in an affirmative manner as the interrogator describes how he thinks the suspect committed the crime and possibly tearing up. In almost all instances, the suspect's eye contact will drop to the floor.

The interrogator should condense the themes to one or two key statements.

Step 7: Presenting the Alternative Question

The alternative question is one in which the suspect is offered two incriminating choices concerning some aspect of committing the crime. Accepting either choice represents the first admission of guilt.

When the suspect displays the above-referred-to indications that he is ready to tell the truth, it is important to make it as easy as possible to obtain the first admission of guilt. The interrogator should not simply ask the suspect at this point, "Did you sell crack?" By asking the question in this manner, we are affording the suspect the opportunity to deny any involvement in the crime. It would also be ineffective to ask the suspect to explain why he was selling drugs. This requires too much effort by the suspect to inaugurate his entire confession. The goal of using an alternative question is to make it as easy as possible for the suspect to begin telling the truth about his commission of the crime.

In formulating the alternative question, one side should describe an understandable reason for committing the crime and the other side should offer a repulsive, inexcusable reason for committing the crime. An example of an alternative question would be, "Was this planned out or did it just happen on the spur-of-the-moment?" Another example would be, "Was this the first time you did something like this or have you been doing this kind of thing for a long time?"

Following the alternative question a supporting statement is presented to the suspect, which encourages him to select one of the offered choices. The supporting statement is part of the presentation of an alternative question. For example, if the suspect is presented with the alternative question, "Was this the first time you did this or have you taken money from the company hundreds of other times?" Immediately following this question would be the supporting statement: "If this was the first time, I could understand that. I think it was the first time, wasn't it?"

Either choice in the alternative question represents the initial admission of guilt. In accepting one side of the alternative question the suspect may simply nod his head or verbalize one word (yes) to admit his guilt. This admission of guilt needs to be developed into a corroborated confession.

It should be made clear that the suspect always has a third choice when presented with an alternative question: namely, that he never committed the crime at all! Also, the alternative question should never threaten consequences or offer promises of leniency.

The following are **improper** alternative question examples:

"Do you want to cooperate with me and tell me what happened, or spend the next five to seven years behind bars?"

"Do you want to be charged with first degree murder, which will mean life in prison, or was this just manslaughter?"

"Are you going to get this straightened out today, or do you want to spend a few days in jail to think about it?"

Step 8: Having the Suspect Orally Relate the Various Details of the Offense

The purpose of this step is to commit the suspect to the crime following his acceptance of the alternative question. This is accomplished by immediately presenting a statement of reinforcement following the suspect's acceptance of the alternative question. The conversation might be something like the following:

Interrogator:	"Frank, have you been selling crack to everyone, kids included or just to adults who happen to approach you? I'm thinking it is just adults who are coming to you, right? They are coming to you, aren't they?" (Alternative question)
Suspect:	"Yeah." Or, the suspect may make a nonverbal acknowledgement by nodding his head.
Interrogator:	"Good Frank, that's what I thought it was all along." (Statement of reinforcement)

This statement of reinforcement validates the suspect's perception of the interrogator as being empathetic and nonjudgmental. It also becomes more difficult for the suspect to recant his initial admission.

Following this statement of support, the suspect is then asked a series of short and brief questions regarding elements of the crime. These questions should be phrased in a way that they require brief answers. The purpose of these questions is to commit the suspect to the crime. Typical initial questions would be: "What happened next?" or "How many times did you do this?" or "Then what did you do?"

Additional questions should follow that essentially corroborate the initial admission of guilt. The interrogator should ask questions that only the actual offender would know the answers to. Examples might be: "What was the (stolen) money used for?" or "Where is the deposit bag that contained the (stolen) money?" or "What was the denomination of the money?" or "What did you do with the (weapon, clothing, money, property)?"

The interrogator should avoid taking written notes during this process. Many suspects view notes as a permanent record of the procedure and may become reluctant to provide additional corroborative information.

Step 9: Elements of Oral and Written Statements

The focus of this step is to reduce the verbal admission to:
1. A statement written and signed by the suspect
2. A statement written by the interrogator and signed by the suspect
3. A tape-recorded statement
4. A video-recorded statement

Chapter 4

Theme Selection Based on the Suspect's Responses to Specific Reid Behavior Analysis Interview (BAI) Questions

Certain Behavior Analysis Interview (BAI) questions are designed not only to discern truth or deception, but also to provide the investigator with insight as to the most effective themes to incorporate into the suspect's interrogation. The BAI questions listed below will only address a few typical responses. After reviewing these responses the investigator will better understand the concept of deriving themes from these specific questions. The following are brief illustrations of BAI behavior-provoking questions that may elicit interrogation theme information.

"Tell me why you wouldn't do this."
Suspect's response: "Because I'm a dedicated employee, not a thief." The theme in this case would be to contrast a dedicated employee who made one mistake with another individual who had no work ethic and only worked with the intent of stealing as much as he could.

"Do you think the person who stole the $1,000 in cash deserves a second chance under any circumstances?"
Suspect's response: "Well if it was the first time that he did something like

this, then perhaps he should be given a second chance." The theme in this example should contrast the interrogator's concern of whether or not the suspect has stolen money only one time or on several previous occasions. Another response to this question may be, "I guess if the person is really sorry for what he did." The theme suggested with this response should be directed to contrasting whether or not the suspect is sorry for what he did.

"What do you think should happen to the person who set the high school on fire?"
Suspect's response: "If he didn't intend to kill anyone and just acted out of frustration then perhaps he should receive counseling." This theme should contrast the suspect's intent to kill versus acting out of frustration and merely engaging in a prank. Another response to this question might be, "I guess if it wasn't his idea and he was just going along with someone else, then I think…" This theme selection should contrast the suspect's idea of planning the offense versus someone else suggesting the idea and the associated peer pressure causing him do something he would not normally do on his own.

"Did you ever just think of having sexual contact with your daughter, not that you would, but did you ever just think about it?"
Suspect's response: "Well, I think that everyone thinks about it, particularly if you have too much to drink." Theme development in this scenario should contrast alcohol as a factor that causes good people to act out of character versus a person who intentionally plans such an act with non-impaired judgment. Another response might be, "Sometimes, when a person is under so much stress, he might think about things that he would normally never consider." This response suggests contrasting the influence of stress on a person's behavior with that of being a sexual predator.

"Did you tell any of your family members about this interview today?"
Suspect's response: "No, not really, I didn't want to worry my wife and besides, she knows that I'm an honest person." Theme development should contrast an honest person making one little mistake versus a dishonest person engaging in this behavior at every possible opportunity. Additionally, the investigator should also consider as a possible concern on the suspect's mind the fear of the consequences he may face if his wife learns about his behavior. The investigator should consider developing interrogation themes that would imply or suggest that his spouse would be more understanding if the crime was committed for a morally acceptable reason.

"If you did this, would you tell anyone?"
Suspect's response: "Probably, because I consider myself a religious person." Since the suspect brought up religion, the investigator's theme selection might suggest that we have all made mistakes, even good people, and the important thing is that we acknowledge our shortcomings and move forward. Another suspect response might be, "No, because people would think that I'm no good." Theme selection in this instance should contrast good people making occasional mistakes versus bad people engaging in this behavior every day.

"What would be the easiest way for someone to do this?"
Suspect's response: "If someone left the keys in his car it would be easy to take the car." Theme selection should blame the victim for carelessness. Or, "If the offender was at the wrong place at the wrong time, sure it could happen." This suggests themes contrasting a situational versus premeditated circumstance.

As is demonstrated from the above examples, it is very important to conduct a non-accusatory interview prior to any interrogation. Some investigators question as to whether or not the interview is even necessary when they have an overwhelming amount of evidence implicating the suspect. It is almost always advisable to conduct an interview for a variety of reasons: establish rapport with the suspect; create the perception by the suspect that the investigator is an objective, non-judgmental individual; and it gives the interrogator an opportunity to develop valuable theme information from the suspect's responses to some of the BAI questions.

Chapter 5

Interrogation Theme Selection and Development

The previous chapter provided some insight into theme selection that can be gained from evaluating the suspect's responses to specific behavior-provoking questions during the BAI. This chapter will explain the anatomy of theme development – namely, how a theme is selected, introduced and developed.

As previously stated, a theme is a persuasive technique designed to reinforce the guilty suspect's existing justifications for committing his crime, thus creating an environment in which the suspect feels more comfortable telling the truth about his criminal activity. By developing the most appropriate themes, the investigator, not the suspect, controls the interrogation environment. Control is obtained during the interrogation by the investigator developing interrogation themes that the suspect can identify with or relate to. When the suspect focuses his attention on the themes he is less likely to engage in denials. Therefore, selecting the most appropriate themes based on motive and the suspect's responses to specific behavior-provoking questions will afford the investigator a greater probability of maintaining control during the interrogation. The structure of theme development is as follows:

Anatomy of Theme Development

1. *The suspect's guilt is presumed.*
   This opinion is based on the suspect's verbal and nonverbal behavior during the interview as well as any evidence and factual information the investigation has revealed.

2. *The investigator attempts to determine motive.*
   The speculation of the crime's motive is based on case facts, evidence, background information, prior crimes of a similar nature and the suspect's interview responses. Additionally, one of the most important questions to ask in preparing for the interrogation is why would someone do this? The determination of motive may direct the investigator to the most appropriate theme selection.

   For example, in a case involving a terrorist act against a U.S. military facility with money as the apparent motive, versus religious beliefs, challenge or revenge, the themes may focus on such ideas as: (1) blaming the suspect's need to provide for his family; (2) blaming the suspect's inability to earn a decent living; (3) blaming someone else for approaching the suspect; (4) blaming the country's poor economy; (5) blaming the suspect's lifestyle as either being out of control or just the opposite, habitually living in poverty; (6) blaming the extreme stress the suspect was under; (7) minimizing the property damage or loss of life; (8) minimizing the frequency the suspect engaged in such behavior; or (9) minimizing the act by contrasting the victim being the military versus innocent civilians.

3. *The question is not if the suspect committed the crime, but rather why.*

As interrogation themes are presented to the suspect, the investigator never asks the suspect whether or not he committed the crime, but rather explains to him why he believes the suspect was motivated to commit the crime.

4. *Reasons and excuses are selected that will serve to psychologically, not legally, justify the suspect's behavior, thus creating an environment where the suspect feels comfortable telling the truth.* These reasons and excuses will generally blame the victim's actions or behavior, something the suspect has already done. For example, an employee that steals money from his employer justifies his theft by perceiving he is underpaid and overworked. He comes to the belief that he is being cheated or victimized and therefore justifies that the money he stole was due him anyway. The parent that physically abuses his child has probably blamed his child's misbehavior for the abuse. The parent may also further rationalize his behavior by convincing himself that he was disciplining the child for his own good, as opposed to engaging in abusive behavior. When the child's misbehavior obviously does not warrant the parent's physically abusive response, the parent tries to rationalize or justify their behavior so that they can psychologically feel comfortable with what they have done.

5. *Minimize the moral seriousness of the suspect's criminal behavior.* There is always something more serious the suspect could have done. The interrogator however, does not imply to the suspect that because his crime is minimized that he will receive a lesser punishment or be relieved of criminal responsibility. Contrasting the suspect that stole $1,000 with another person that stole $10,000 creates a more comfortable environment for the suspect. The suspect still knows that he was wrong for stealing the $1,000 but feels better knowing that he did not steal $10,000. Another

example of minimization might be using time bars to minimize the psychological aspects of the suspect's behavior. For example, it may appear difficult to minimize the behavior of a 32-year-old serial rapist who has committed 20 rapes during the past five years. However, the investigator might develop themes which contrast a situation in which these activities (20 rapes) only occurred during the last five years of his life, as opposed to someone who has been engaging in this type of behavior for the last 15 years of his adult life. The suspect may be complimented for living many years as an exemplary person and that something of a devastating nature must have occurred five years ago to cause the suspect to act totally out of character. The theme may be focused on what that event was, thereby attempting to further minimize the moral seriousness of the suspect's horrific criminal acts.

6. *Develop personal stories (third-person themes) of other*
   individuals committing similar but much more serious crimes.
   The investigator should also consider developing third-person themes. Third-person themes are stories about other individuals that have committed a similar but much more serious crime and the extenuating circumstances that caused the behavior. These third-person themes can be real or fictitious. They might be about a story being presented in the media, a similar case the investigator worked on, or a hypothetical example of the investigator himself. In developing the latter, the dialogue of the investigator regarding the theft of $1,000 might be as follows: "Nicole, let me tell you that I consider myself an honest person, just as I believe you are a basically an honest person. If, however, I was in your situation, where the need and opportunity were present, I don't know how I might react. If I had to purchase schoolbooks as you did, had no money and came across money

left out on a desk, I don't know what I would do. That is what I think happened here. I think two ingredients, need and opportunity, presented themselves, which caused you to act out of character and do something that you normally would never do." This third-person theme does not tell the suspect that the investigator would commit the crime but it is suggested that anyone, even the investigator, is capable of making a bad decision. This approach not only minimizes the suspect's actions, but also, more importantly, causes the suspect to view the investigator as being understanding and non-judgmental.

7. *Maintain a sympathetic and empathetic approach.*

It is imperative that throughout the entire interrogation, despite how repulsive the crime might be, the investigator conveys that he understands how and why the suspect committed the offense. The impression to the suspect is that the investigator understands how anyone could have done what the suspect did. This empathy and concern exhibited toward the suspect's behavior tends to perceptually minimize the uniqueness of the suspect's behavior as well as change the suspect's perception of the investigator. The suspect may gradually sense the investigator is not an adversary, but rather a person that truly understands the unique circumstances that caused the crime.

8. *Repeat, repeat, and repeat.*

Most suspects are listening to a fraction of what the investigator is saying during the interrogation. Suspects focus on the consequences of their behavior: loss of job, jail, embarrassment, loss of social standing or restitution. Therefore, after various themes have been presented with no resulting admission, it is essential to repeat the primary themes. The suspect's behavior during theme development should guide the investigator during this process. As themes are repeated, if the suspect exhibits physical barriers, lack of eye contact or little interest, the interrogator must be willing to divorce that specific theme and attempt another. Once the suspect begins to accept a specific theme, the suspect's behavior will generally change to appear more receptive. The suspect begins to make eye contact, nod in agreement and no longer denies his involvement in the crime.

9. *Avoid allowing the suspect to make long statements or explanations; try to maintain control of the interrogation.*
   During theme development most suspects will try to gain control by denying the crime or offering objections to disrupt the interrogation flow. As described in Steps 3 and 4, the interrogator should attempt to discourage denials and immediately return to the development of the theme, and in the case of an objection, use that statement to further reinforce the theme message.

10. *The objective of the theme development stage is to set the foundation for the first admission of guilt.*
    Most suspects will first acknowledge involvement in the crime with a nod of the head or a verbal acknowledgment to one of the choices offered in the alternative question. The alternative question is typically the logical extension of the theme. When a suspect is about to admit his guilt in response to the alternative question, for example, "Is this the first time you took money or have you been taking it for a long time?" it is very important to remember that an acknowledgement that this was the first time the suspect stole money is not a full confession but rather an admission of guilt. Following the initial admission of guilt the investigator must be very deliberate in developing the full details of the suspect's criminal behavior as well as corroborating details of the crime.

During theme development, it is very important that the investigator not make statements that imply inevitable consequences (threats) or make statements that could be perceived as promises of leniency.

The interrogation themes discussed in this section and for each offense in the following chapter are by no means the only themes that may be developed during the interrogation nor are they necessarily mutually exclusive to different crimes.   They are intended to provide the investigator with ideas that may be modified or expanded upon during the interrogation. Additionally, very different crimes may share the same basic motive – themes for one offense may overlap another offense. For example, if a husband kills his wife for the insurance money (financial/greed motive) or a business owner sets fire to his building for the insurance money, in both instances similar themes may be developed. The interrogation themes for the homicide may involve blaming the victim for not contributing emotionally and financially to the relationship, whereas in the arson the theme would blame the fact that based on the time and money invested by the owner, the economic conditions did not generate an adequate profit.

In some criminal acts the real motive of the offender's behavior may be very offensive or difficult to morally excuse. Therefore, some themes do not address the true motive of the crime. In the case of a child molester committing crimes simply because of his own sexual preference and with no regard whatsoever for the victim's physical or emotional well-being, it may be too difficult for the offender himself to accept or to perceive that others would understand why he committed these acts. In this example, perhaps the most appropriate interrogation theme may be to focus on the idea that alcohol, drugs or stress may have caused the suspect's behavior, as opposed to the real reason why he committed the crime. Additionally, the suspect's behavior could be minimized by contrasting the type of sexual acts that occurred or the number of times that the suspect had engaged in this activity with more serious sexual activities or frequency. In either case, once the suspect accepts and acknowledges the theme, an initial admission is obtained.

In preparing the interrogation strategy and possible themes that can be used, it is critically important to consider the possible motivation of the offender. If the investigator believes that an employee's motive for stealing money from his employer was to pay an unusual family expense such as his child's college tuition, themes should contrast that true motive with another much more reprehensible motive. In this example, themes for the employee who steals money to fund college expenses may be:

1. Blame the unusual family expense of unexpected college tuition
2. Suggest the suspect was counting on his child receiving a scholarship
3. Suggest the suspect wanted the best education as possible for his child
4. Blame the suspect for underestimating the cost of college education
5. Blame the employer for paying low wages or lack of promotions
6. Blame the poor controls of the employer
7. Blame the high cost of living
8. Compliment the suspect for accepting responsibility for his financial obligations
9. Suggest the crime as being out of character
10. Suggest the employee may have eventually wanted to repay the stolen money

Interrogation themes need to be expanded upon by the interrogator. Simply saying to the suspect, "I think that you took the money to pay for your child's college expense, didn't you?" would probably be met with a denial from the suspect. The following is an example of how the interrogator would develop themes for the employee that stole money from his employer to pay for college expenses.

(Step 1 – The Positive Confrontation)

Interrogator: "Dan, in this file I have the results of our investigation regarding the missing $15,000 deposit from your employer. Dan, the results clearly indicate that you took the missing $15,000 deposit."

(The suspect is allowed to voice a denial.)

Interrogator: "Dan, as I said, the results clearly indicate that you took the deposit. What I would like to do is sit down with you to see if we can get this thing explained."

(Step 2 – Theme Development)

Interrogator: "Dan, I know that you are an exemplary employee and would never do anything to intentionally take advantage of your employer. However, sometimes a need and opportunity present itself that can cause a person to do something that he would normally never do. I think that is what happened here. I think you needed extra money to pay your daughter's college expenses, and we all know how expensive that can be. There is tuition, room and board, proper clothing, a cell phone, a computer, a printer, software and books; the list goes on forever. Dan, the need was present. The opportunity was also present; you have access to the company's cash deposits. Combining these two ingredients, need and opportunity, many times results in causing a good, hard-working person to do something out of character. That is exactly what I think happened with you."

(Step 3 – Denials)

Suspect: "But I didn't take the money, I swear."

Interrogator: "Dan, there is no doubt that you took the money. Let me just finish what I was saying."

(Interrogator returns to themes) "Perhaps you were counting on the college to help defray the costs by providing some type of scholarship or loans that it failed to offer. You now have a difficult decision to make – find additional income or not allow your daughter to attend such a good school. You know as a good father that not allowing your daughter to get a good education will affect her for the rest of her entire life. You want her to have opportunities that you didn't have. You, like most really good parents, want the best for your children.

"When you combine your need for money with the fact that your employer did not properly secure the daily cash deposits, a solution for your problem presented itself. The temptation was just too great. You had access and due to the stress that you were under, you gave in to temptation and took the deposit. Additionally, I know that you are not being paid a huge salary. I think that if you were being paid properly or had been given a few more promotions you would never have taken the money. Am I right? You know I'm right."

(Step 4 – Objections)

Suspect: "I'm an honest person, why would I take the deposit?"

Interrogator: "I'm glad you said that. I know you are an honest person. If you were a dishonest person this would not have been the first time you had taken money. But I think it was the first time, which tells me that you are an honest guy that made one mistake. If you were dishonest there would have been all kinds of money missing."

(Interrogator returns to themes) "The company should have had better controls and not left the deposits on the manager's desk. You and I both know that if the deposit was in the safe you wouldn't be here. I don't think that you would have broken into the safe, would you? I don't think you would have."

(Step 5 – Procurement and Retention of Suspect's Attention)

The interrogator gradually begins moving closer to the suspect and begins to shorten themes.

Interrogator: "But the deposit was easily accessible and you gave in to temptation and took it. I don't think that you got the job to do something like this, but I don't know that for sure. That is why I'm talking to you. I think this was more spur-of-the-moment and you simply acted out of character as opposed to something that you had planned from the very first day you started with the company."

(Step 6 – Handling the Suspect's Passive Mood)

The interrogator observes the suspect becoming less vocal and nonverbally resigned; the suspect lacks frontal alignment; the barriers begin to fall open; the suspect moves into a slumped over position and is unable to look the interrogator in the eye.

(Step 7 – Alternatives)

Interrogator: "Dan, I think this was out of character, wasn't it? I don't think you are a dishonest guy, are you? I think you acted on the spur-of-the-moment, didn't you? You did, didn't you?"
Suspect: "Yeah."

Once the suspect acknowledges the act, the interrogator has obtained the first *admission* of guilt. It then becomes necessary to orally commit the suspect to the crime by *obtaining details* (Step 8). The details in this example might be: the denomination of the money, the exact location where the deposit was stolen, the exact time of the theft, how the deposit was arranged or packaged, acknowledgment and receipts of what the money was used for, etc. Once the details of the offense have been obtained, the interrogator then converts the verbal admission into a recorded *confession* (Step 9).

Offenders do not always commit crimes for good reasons. An employee who steals from his employer to purchase illegal drugs realizes he does not have a "good" reason for his behavior. This offender also believes that there is no benefit in telling the truth since, in his perception, no one will understand why he committed the crime. The suspect that commits a crime for a "bad" reason is more reluctant to tell the truth because an admission would compound two negative acts – stealing money and using illegal drugs.   The interrogator must always remember that when developing themes, there is always something more serious that the suspect could have done; there is always a morally acceptable excuse for the suspect's behavior.

Themes that accomplish these goals for the employee that steals money to buy illegal drugs may focus on:

1. Blaming drug dependency as being an uncontrollable addiction much like legal addictions such as gambling, being a compulsive worker, drinking, cigarette smoking, etc.
2. Mentioning other good people that made mistakes as a result of their compulsive behavior – Betty Ford, the former President's wife using drugs but then founding a drug rehabilitation clinic, turning a negative into a positive
3. Suggest the drug usage did not occur on the job and it did not adversely affect the suspect's work performance
4. Compliment the suspect for only taking money necessary to supplement the cost of the drugs versus taking money to gamble, take extravagant vacations, etc.
5. Compliment the suspect for being an exemplary employee
6. Blame the stress that the suspect is under (job or family)
7. Blame the employer for not providing a proper drug rehabilitation program
8. Blame the suspect's fear of loss of job for not seeking help
9. Blame the suspect's lifestyle – being around people that commonly use drugs suggesting peer pressure
10. Contrast either the amount of drug or the type of drug being used

Common Themes to Crimes

In addition to blaming the victim's actions or behavior for the suspect committing the offense, there are some themes that an interrogator can develop with the suspect that are common to many crimes. External factors such as peer pressure, alcohol, or drugs and stress become the precipitators of many offenses. Therefore, this section will provide the reader with examples of such theme dialogue.

Peer pressure as a theme

"Nicole, a lot of times we do things that we would normally never do simply because we are with individuals that influence our behavior. Take me for instance, why do you think I had my first cigarette? Because I was with some friends that were smoking and they gave me my first cigarette. Why do you think I had my first drink? Again, because I was with some friends that were drinking and they handed me the beer. I just went along, pretending to be cool, without really thinking about it, like most people would do.

"I can see a person being at the wrong place at the wrong time and someone tells him how easy it would be to take someone's car, particularly when the keys were left in the ignition. This entire conversation takes place by your friends Kristen and Genna and you just listen. The more you listen, the more desensitized you become and the less serious the theft seems. Why? Because having someone tell you how easy it would be to drive away with such a nice car almost normalizes taking the car, particularly since it was only for a joyride anyway.

"That is what I think happened here. I think you were at the wrong place at the wrong time. I also think that if Kristen and Genna had not pointed out the car with the keys in the ignition, you would not have taken the car on your own. I don't think this was your idea; in fact, I think that if your friends Kristen and Genna were not with you, you wouldn't be here now! Am I right? This wasn't your idea, was it?"

Alcohol/Drugs as a theme

"Brian, I think the reason you did this was because of the alcohol you had that night. There isn't a person I know that hasn't had one too many drinks that has caused him to do something he would normally not have done. I'm not here to be judgmental, but the fact is that people act differently when they consume alcohol.

"A friend of mine, Bill, is normally a low key, shy guy. It seems that when he has one too many tequilas, he changes to a very outgoing, talkative guy. It's like watching a thermometer on a sunny day. As the sun gets higher in the sky, the temperature keeps getting higher and higher. At first the temperature seems comfortable, even pleasant. But as the day grows longer things begin to change. It no longer is comfortable. In fact, it becomes unbearable. It's the same with Bill's behavior.

"The first drink makes you feel pretty good. As you have a few more drinks, you feel even better. However, the more you drink, the more out of character you become. The alcohol at first tasted good and made you feel good. The more you drink, the worse you feel. You can no longer deal rationally with conflict. The alcohol influences every decision that you now make. Normally, you may weigh the pros and cons of important decisions. But after one too many drinks, there is no pro or con. There is only one way, your way and not enough time to do it. That is what I think happened here, no thought of what was right or wrong, just doing what had to be done. I think if you weren't drinking, this would never have happened! Right?"

Stress as a theme

"I find that each person has his own breaking point. I believe that I am an average guy just like you. Sometimes the stress of a situation can make a good, hard-working person make a mistake and do something that he normally wouldn't do. I'll share such a situation that happened to me. I first have to tell you that I'm really ashamed to tell you this.

"I just got home from a business trip and was dead tired. It was 2:00 in the morning. I was so tired that I was shaking. I got in bed and after an hour or so of tossing and turning I just began to fall asleep. At that precise moment, our eight-month-old daughter in the next bedroom begins to cry. I don't mean a normal cry, but a certain cry that goes on and on. To me it begins sounding like the shriek and shrill of fingernails being scratched slowly across a chalkboard. I couldn't take it. I was so stressed out that I turned to my wife Jean who was sound asleep. Just looking at her in such a relaxed state made me hot! She'd been sleeping all night and didn't have a care in the world. It wasn't fair. Why didn't she deal with this situation? I began to hyperventilate, getting angrier and angrier. I couldn't take it any longer. That's when I turned to my wife Jean and said, 'You better get up and shut that kid up because if I go into her room, I'm going to pull her out of the crib and throw her in the dresser drawer!'

"Thank goodness my wife calmed me and took care of our daughter. The point I'm making here is that stress made me say something that I truly wasn't proud of, in fact, something that I never would have believed I would have said. But more importantly, I had a spouse that quite possibly prevented something very serious from happening.

"I think that if you had a spouse that calmed you, you would not have shaken your child as you did. In fact, your spouse only created more stress by not dealing with the situation. I think that you are a good dad, but I think the stress of the situation caused you to act out of character and do something that you truly regret. I don't think you did this because you hated your daughter; in fact, I'm totally convinced that you love your daughter very much. I just think it was the stress of the moment, right?"

It should be pointed out that personal stories that the interrogator chooses to tell about himself do not have to be the truth.

Chapter 6

Crimes and Related Themes

This section contains over 50 crimes and more than 1,600 interrogation theme options for the investigator to consider. Most of the crimes presented contain a brief example of an interrogation so as to illustrate the theme development. Interrogation themes are not necessarily mutually exclusive; themes for one offense may clearly be viable for another seemingly unrelated crime. The theme development, however, is abbreviated for the purpose of incorporating as many examples as possible. The examples of potential theme material for each of the types of crimes described in this chapter provide a core of ideas for the monologue process (*Step 2, Theme Development*) which begins after *Step 1, The Positive Confrontation* and culminates with the first admission of guilt in *Step 7, The Alternative Question*.

Once the suspect accepts one of the alternative options in *Step 7*, the investigator then proceeds to develop details of the offense in *Step 8*. After the initial admission has been developed into a corroborated confession, in *Step 9* the verbal statement will be converted into a written or recorded statement.

Animal Cruelty

The following interrogation themes may be supplemented by certain themes noted under child physical abuse, elder abuse or domestic violence. The primary motives involving animal cruelty would include anger, stress or frustration, misbehavior of the animal, alcohol/drug abuse by the suspect and financial (for example, the suspect unable to afford proper training or medical treatment for the animal).

A. Blame the animal for:

1. Misbehavior such as inability to be house-trained, biting, aggressiveness, etc.
2. Requiring excessive medical treatment, resulting in unexpected expenses
3. Making too much noise, resulting in neighbor's complaints
4. Running away
5. Suggest that when the suspect obtained the animal, he was misinformed about the animal's training, intelligence or temperament

B. Blame outside factors or minimize the suspect's behavior:

1. Stress – neighbors complaining, loss of job, divorce, marital separation, etc.
2. Alcohol or drugs
3. Peer pressure
4. Inability to afford the upkeep for the animal
5. Suggest the suspect was raised to treat animals in this manner
6. Suggest the suspect's intent was tough love to correct a problem versus cruelty
7. Suggest the suspect overreacted to a situation

8. Contrast an isolated incident versus a pattern of behavior
9. Exaggerate what the suspect could have done
10. Impulse

Example: Eric got upset with his dog Thunder and intentionally stepped on him, breaking his leg.

"I think what happened Eric, is that Thunder's behavior simply became frustrating, causing you to act out of character. I can see by the newspapers around the house that Thunder was just plain difficult to house-train. In addition, I saw the marks on your furniture as well as the shrubbery outside that he was chewing on. Sometimes, we overreact to situations not because we are mean, but simply due to frustration. There is no doubt that the injuries to Thunder were not caused by accident; they were intentional. However, I do not know if the injuries are the result of an isolated incident or if you have a pattern of this behavior.

"We discovered the injuries early enough to be corrected, which is very good. The fact that Thunder was not killed or tortured tells me that you really like Thunder but acted on impulse as opposed to a planned-out manner. I also know that you have been laid off work for the last several months. That has to be really hard, Eric. As I look at the big picture, you seem like a good guy that out of frustration, due to the loss of your job, combined with Thunder being difficult to house-train, caused you to act out of character and step on his leg. My concern is this, were you trying to kill Thunder or were you just trying to teach him a lesson? You weren't trying to kill or torture him, were you? It was just out of frustration, wasn't it?"

Arson Themes

Theme selection for arson investigations will address the primary motives with suggested themes for each.

A. Vandalism:

1. Blame affected judgment due to alcohol, boredom, peer pressure, etc.
2. Blame the fire department; suggest the damage would never have been so extensive had the department responded in a more timely manner
3. Blame the weather conditions for accelerating or not extinguishing the fire
4. Blame the property as being an eyesore or in need of significant repair
5. Minimize the uniqueness of the crime by suggesting that no one was seriously injured or that loss of life did not occur
6. Minimize the dollar loss
7. Suggest the act was a spur-of-the-moment decision; highlight the fact that no accelerant was used
8. Contrast starting the fire on a dare versus a much more serious motive such as arson for profit or crime concealment
9. Contrast a small, contained fire versus burning an entire building as well as surrounding structures
10. Suggest first-time experimenting with fire

B. Spite/Revenge:

1. Blame the action or behavior the victim displayed toward the suspect, possibly suggesting racial prejudice, anti-Semitism, cheating, etc.

2. Suggest an act of frustration
3. Blame the suspect's uncontrolled emotions toward the victim – anger, frustration, jealousy, revenge, hate, etc.
4. Blame the influence of alcohol and/or drugs
5. Blame the suspect's belief that the structure burned was in direct contrast with the suspect's moral or religious beliefs – abortion clinics, church fires, etc. – the church/abortion clinic set on fire was "brainwashing" people or fostered a "cult" mentality
6. Blame peer pressure
7. Contrast one time versus many
8. Contrast intent to scare the victim as opposed to harming or murdering them
9. Contrast spite/revenge motive with that of a more serious motive, such as arson for profit
10. Minimize the amount of accelerant used, suggesting intent was not to cause the amount of damage that resulted

C. Arson for profit/financially motivated:

1. Blame accomplice for suggesting the idea
2. Blame the insurance company for overinsuring the property or contents
3. Blame the insurance company for cheating the suspect in past claims, suggesting the intent was to recoup prior losses
4. Blame poor business/income for draining the suspect's life savings, suggesting intent was to "break even" financially
5. Blame unfair competition for causing loss of business income
6. Blame amount of time needed to devote to business/property, suggesting this was an act of desperation
7. Blame family pressure for devoting too much time to the business
8. Suggest fire was set to help family or loved ones, e.g. the suspect

was paid to fight fires on a part-time basis and needed a full-time job's income

9. Minimize number of fires started
10. Minimize offense by contrasting the suspect's poor preparation with that of a highly sophisticated, premeditated arson
11. Contrast greed versus need (breaking even)
12. Suggest initial fire was legitimate and the suspect saw an opportunity to add accelerant

D. Concealing another crime:

1. Burglary/Embezzlement – blame the suspect's specific need such as bills, drug dependency, nuisance from creditors, etc.
2. Homicide – the primary theme should initially focus on obtaining the first admission to arson as opposed to homicide – describe intentions for starting fire: to show that the apartment was a firetrap, to get new furniture, to collect the insurance money, etc. Following an admission to the arson, the interrogator should then re-interrogate the suspect using homicide themes.
3. Blame pressure and stress for making the suspect act out of character
4. Minimize intent, suggesting purpose was to destroy documents versus a building
5. Suggest intent of fire was to conceal an act of wrongdoing (embezzlement, fraud, burglary, rape, etc.), as opposed to taking someone's life
6. Exaggerate what the suspect attempted to concealed in the arson: one year of documents as opposed to ten years of documents, a premeditated homicide versus a homicide committed with little or no premeditation
7. Suggest someone giving the suspect this idea
8. Suggest the suspect acted out of desperation, as opposed to

detailed scheming
9. Blame alcohol/drug usage
10. Contrast this one fire with several fires that occurred

E. Pyromania:

1. Suggest acceptable motive or initial intent for starting the fire, such as keeping warm, curiosity to see if something would burn, a controlled fire that got out of hand, etc.
2. Blame irresistible impulses – the obsessive-compulsive personality is fully aware of his urges to engage in unwanted behavior, just as the smoker is fully aware of the risk he takes, but nonetheless gives in to his urge
3. Blame stress
4. Minimize the number of fires set
5. Suggest suspect was unable to cope with his emotions
6. Blame sheer boredom

F. Attention-motivated arsons:

1. Address the specific need directly – need to reassure parent/spousal love, need to validate workplace value, etc.
2. Blame stressful events – loss of job, family member, bankruptcy, etc.
3. Blame easy access to accelerant/explosives or knowledge gained from books and Internet
4. Suggest the act was not intended to hurt anyone but rather to bring to the forefront a seemingly irresolvable problem
5. As a last resort, in an attempt to obtain admissions from the suspect to acknowledge causing the fire, suggest the fire was accidentally started. If the suspect accepts the accident theme, re-interrogate the suspect attempting to obtain his specific intent.

Example: Rick sets fire to his restaurant to collect insurance money.

"Rick, I think the reason you set fire to your restaurant was to simply break even. I know that you have tried your hardest for the last four years to earn a decent living. However, the big restaurant chains have been opening all around you. You don't have the ability to buy your food or supplies at the much lower cost that your competitors do. So what do you do? As a result of the unfair competition, you have to work harder and stay open longer and lower your prices. You can only do that for so long. The more time you spend on your business means less time you have to spend with your family. Not only are you under a great deal of financial pressure but now you are compounding that with family pressure.

"When a good, hard-working person is faced with so many unusual circumstances, that person can sometimes do something totally uncharacteristic. That is what I think happened here. By the way, we know that you are an honest person because for the last four years you have devoted yourself to nurturing and developing a community business. If, on the other hand, the fire started just weeks or months after you opened the restaurant we would be suspicious of your intentions. By the fact that this happened four years after opening, then that tells us something. What that something is, is that you are an honest guy that saw no other way out. That is what I think happened here. I don't think you were trying to do something really bad like killing someone in a fire, or concealing years of financial records where you were cheating on your income taxes. What I think happened was the result of stress, family and financial pressure. I also don't think that you wanted to profit by lying about additional contents burned in the fire. I think you just wanted to break even, right? You weren't trying to hurt anyone or make a false profit. You just wanted out of a no-win situation, right?"

Attention-Seeking Crime Themes

Some individuals seek attention to validate their self-worth by committing unthinkable crimes. Fortunately, most people are emotionally mature and satisfy their need for attention in a more positive manner: by striving to be an A student, excelling in the workplace, establishing good family values, accepting increasing responsibility, etc. The attention seeker's behavior tends to compensate for his low self-esteem or feelings of inadequacy.

These themes are divided into three groups. One set of themes focuses on acts against other individuals – as an example, Munchausen Syndrome by Proxy. The second set of themes focuses on false claims regarding the suspect himself, and the third set of themes is directed toward crimes against property, for example, the volunteer firefighter or security officer setting fires then extinguishing them for the purpose of control, power or recognition.

A. **Actions against other individuals (as an example – Munchausen Syndrome by Proxy):**

1. Contrast causing harm for attention versus causing harm out of malice
2. Contrast loving versus hating the victim – suggesting the victim was simply the messenger for the suspect's attention seeking
3. Contrast harming versus murder
4. Compliment the suspect for getting prompt medical attention for the victim
5. Contrast causing pain to the victim versus not causing pain
6. Contrast withholding medication versus giving the wrong medication
7. Contrast one-time incident versus several

8. Suggest the suspect as being a misunderstood, loving, caring person
9. Suggest the injuries are unjustly being exaggerated
10. Suggest the suspect was glad the crime was discovered
11. Suggest the suspect exaggerated existing injuries
12. Suggest someone else's idea
13. Suggest the suspect was calling for help
14. Blame the victim for having a terminal illness (in a homicide)
15. Blame the victim for being in constant pain (in a homicide)
16. Blame the victim for not being able to pay for proper medical treatment
17. Blame the victim for not having family to help him (in a homicide)
18. Blame rejection by peers
19. Minimize the injury
20. If death occurs, suggest intent was to hurt, not kill

B. Actions against oneself, i.e., falsely reporting being raped, robbed, mugged, abducted:

1. Blame someone else or the media for giving the suspect this idea
2. Blame the job, military, family, friends, school, etc. for not providing opportunities or the ability to obtain proper levels of recognition
3. Blame others for constantly bragging, getting all the glory, being the center of attention, being in the newspaper or on television, etc.
4. Blame the stress of the job, family, military, school, etc.
5. Blame the suspect's parents for never giving proper recognition
6. Suggest the suspect could not live up to his parents' expectations
7. Blame the claim as having occurred as the result of a physical or emotional disorder such as alcoholism, drug abuse, depression, paranoia, etc.

8. Blame the suspect's immaturity or age
9. Blame the suspect's role model as always being perfect and the center of attention
10. Compliment the suspect for not hurting or falsely identifying another individual
11. Suggest the repeated acts were actually committed with the idea of calling for help, hoping to get caught
12. Contrast one time versus several
13. Contrast time bars – one year versus ten years of this behavior
14. Contrast spur-of-the-moment versus planned out
15. Contrast causing a permanent versus a temporary injury
16. Intent was to observe a reaction
17. Intent was for love, affection or attention
18. Exaggerating an existing illness versus creating an illness
19. Suggest intent was financial, i.e., false robbery to get a raise, promotion or recognition

C. Actions against property:

These crimes are generally committed by inadequate, frustrated, ineffectual individuals – examples might be the security officer or volunteer firefighter setting, then discovering the fire for recognition, or an employee putting a granular substance in the workplace then discovering the foreign substance, wanting people to believe it was anthrax or some other seriously contagious chemical.

1. Minimize the frequency of offenses (one time versus many times)
2. Minimize the extent of damage
3. Blame society for demeaning or never giving the suspect recognition – being critical of the suspect's job, level of education, lifestyle, etc.
4. Blame alcohol or drugs

5.   Blame others for contributing to the suspect's low self-image
6.   Blame a recent stressful event in the suspect's life, i.e., death of spouse, loss of job, failing in school, etc.
7.   Blame the poor security thus facilitating the ease of committing the crime
8.   Blame peer pressure
9.   Blame boredom
10. Blame dysfunctional family
11. Blame lack of opportunities
12. Blame inadequate education resulting in limiting promotions
13. Blame the suspect's constant disappointments
14. Contrast planned out versus spur-of-the-moment
15. Suggest the suspect's behavior is "copycat" as opposed to the initiator
16. Suggest suspect's intent was to observe the excitement resulting from the behavior, wanting to see people's reactions
17. Suggest intent was not to hurt anyone, but rather just be in the public eye, i.e., the glory grabber
18. Suggest the act was a call for help, since the act was not well planned and easily discernible that it was fabricated
19. Suggest the suspect committed the crime with the intent to gain a promotion or recognition

Example: Mark, an employee recently passed over for promotion, discovered a powdered substance in the men's washroom at work. The media has recently reported legitimate findings of anthrax discovered in mail facilities.

"Mark, the substance that you discovered was verified as nothing more than a sugar substitute. We know that you were the person that actually put the powder in the washroom and reported it to security. However, our concern is, is this something that was simply the result of frustration and disappointment in the workplace or was this the start of a sinister plan? In other words, was this going to escalate into something more serious, such as the actual placement of hazardous material or the setting of a fire or explosion? I'm thinking Mark, this was more spontaneous. The reason I'm saying that is because the powder you claim that you discovered is the same sugar substitute that we have in our cafeteria. That tells me that this was something you decided to do here at work, which is obviously more spontaneous. If, however, you had brought something from home, then that would have told me that you had planned out this act.

"I also think this was the result of extreme frustration for not being promoted. I know that you have been an exemplary employee who was really counting on the promotion. What is also obvious is that I don't think that you wanted to hurt anyone. If you were mean and a genuine threat, the substance or incident would have been very serious, even life threatening. You didn't start a fire that caused damage to the company or worse yet injured people. The reason you didn't is because you are not a bad guy. You're a guy that did something he now regrets. Right? It is for all these reasons that we need to resolve this matter now. If this was the result of frustration, not meaning to hurt anyone, spontaneous and an act of desperation, we need to know that.   Or, was it to escalate into something more serious?   Was this the result of legitimate frustration by not being promoted? I think it was just out of frustration, wasn't it Mark?"

Auto Theft Themes

A. Blame the victim for:

1.   Leaving keys in the car
2.   Leaving the car running or unlocked

3. Leaving valuables in the car, creating a tempting situation, i.e., cell phone, briefcase, camera, wallet, purse, etc.
4. Parking in a questionable area or neighborhood
5. Not having an alarm system or a kill switch that shuts off the engine's ignition system
6. Not having a steering wheel lock preventing air bag theft or a collar (a device that prevents the steering column from being tampered with)
7. Not etching the VIN onto car parts
8. Having an expensive car, one the suspect could never afford
9. Having expensive stereo components
10. Having expensive wheels, tires or other unique equipment

B. Minimize the suspect's intent by contrasting:

1. Joyride versus using the car in a felony such as a rape, drive-by shooting, burglary, etc.
2. One time versus several
3. Contrast detailed fraud such as selling car outright by changing VIN numbers versus only selling parts of the car
4. No one was physically threatened
5. Suggest intent was the challenge
6. Suggest car was stolen for a joyride versus to obtain garage door opener with intent to burglarize victim's home or commit some other heinous crime inside the home
7. Suggest suspect needed car parts for himself versus selling parts
8. Suggest suspect needed car for personal or job-related reasons
9. Suggest intent was to return vehicle
10. Suggest intent was to help others such as family or friends versus self

C. Other factors:

1. Peer pressure
2. Alcohol/drugs
3. Suggest victim has insurance – stressing that this is essentially a victimless act
4. Blame the suspect's unemployment
5. Suggest thrill and excitement
6. Situational, spur-of-the-moment
7. Gang initiation
8. Suggest an act of revenge against the victim
9. Blame the weather - cold, hot, rainy, etc.
10. Suggest suspect only participated as the accomplice

Example: Lou steals Dan's new Lincoln Aviator that was parked on a side street next to a parking lot during a Chicago White Sox ballgame. Lou is caught driving the car but says a guy named Billy that he knows from his neighborhood allowed him to use the car.

"Lou, I think the reason that you took that Aviator was because the owner, a guy named Dan, was too cheap to park it in the secured ballpark parking lot. Plus, he never took precautions like putting a security device on the steering wheel or even bothered to have an alarm or ignition cut-off installed. The police stopped you driving the car during the seventh inning of the game. What that tells me is that you felt safe driving the car because you thought the owner would have stayed all nine innings of the game. Also, there was no guy named Billy that let you use the car. You said that because you had no other choice. But because the owner left the game early, he discovered the car missing before you could bring it back.

"I also think that it was a really nice car and you knew that you couldn't afford such an expensive car and just wanted to see how it handled. Maybe you just planned on driving around your neighborhood letting your friends become jealous seeing you behind the wheel of such a nice car.

"A lot of people that I've talked to in similar situations have taken cars not just for joy-rides or to show off, but to bring to chop shops or use during the commission of very serious crimes. If you were going to use the car in a drive-by or rape or something like that, then I could see your concern. However, Lou, if you simply took the car because the owner made it easy, and because you knew how long it would be before he discovered it missing, then we need to know that. I also think that if Dan had parked his car in the parking lot, you would have never taken it! Right? This was just the result of a nice car, not secured, being parked on the street. You weren't going to bring the car to a chop shop, were you? I'm thinking this was something that was really brought on by Dan not taking proper measures to protect his car, right Lou?"

Blackmail Themes

Blackmail or extortion occurs when property or money is obtained through the use of oral or written threats. Threats can be physical harm to the victim or his family. The harm can be non-physical such as attacking the victim's reputation or his ability to earn a living. Therefore, themes should be selected that address physical and emotional threats as well as whether or not money or property had exchanged hands.

1. If the victim was physically harmed, attempt to minimize the injuries by contrasting greater injuries, sustaining permanent disabilities or death

2. Minimize the threat of the extortion, contrast harming the victim's reputation versus physical harm, or contrast a threat to the adult

victim versus against the victim's children

3. Minimize by suggesting the verbal/physical threat was not intended to have been carried out

4. Minimize by suggesting no one was kidnapped or, if kidnapped, not harmed

5. Compliment the suspect for not revealing sensitive information regarding the victim

6. Suggest the suspect changed his mind and decided to stop the extortion – which is validated as no money or property changed hands

7. Suggest the situation started as a bad joke but unfortunately escalated

8. Contrast large demand versus reasonable demand

9. Contrast one time versus several

10. Contrast the suspect's behavior with that of a serious offender such as a serial murderer, rapist, arsonist, etc.

11. Blame the victim for engaging in illegal or morally questionable activities

12. Blame the victim's prior negative behavior towards the blackmailer/extortionist, i.e., not giving recognition, pay raises, treating badly, etc.

13. Blame affected judgment, i.e., alcohol, stress, drugs, peer pressure

14. Blame a combination of unfortunate financial situations, suggesting this behavior as an act of desperation resulting from a loss of job, unusual family expenses, family pressure, etc.

15. Blame another individual for providing the suspect information necessary to commit the act of blackmail/extortion

16. Blame greed versus malice

17. Blame the suspect's prior criminal record – suggesting no one would provide employment to the suspect

18. Blame the carelessness of the victim for allowing himself to be

victimized

19. Blame the victim for exaggerating the threats
20. Blame the victim's poor security

Example: Art, a disgruntled former employee of Dr. Smith attempts to extort money from Dr. Smith by threatening to report Dr. Smith for violating proper medical procedures by having pre-signed prescription forms completed by his receptionist.

"Art, we understand that Dr. Smith is a very demanding boss to work for. We also understand that you worked for him for three years with no real problems. We also know that you demanded $10,000 in return for not reporting the doctor about his use of pre-signed prescriptions.   There are really two issues, Art.   One is the doctor's behavior.   That will be addressed with a thorough investigation.   The other issue is your behavior.   As you probably know by now, we are aware that you are attempting to get money from the doctor for not turning him in.   As you know, that is illegal to do.   But what we are concerned with is not whether or not you are trying to get money from the doctor, but rather is this something you have been doing with regularity in the past.   Ten thousand dollars is not a life savings for the doctor but for some people it is.   Our concern is have you been doing this to every employer you have worked for?   Our other concern, therefore, is if this was a one-time occurrence motivated out of frustration due to the high demands and expectations of the doctor, or simply greed.   If you are trying to ruin the doctor's career for the sole purpose of making money, then that is just plain wrong.   On the other hand, if you really were a hard worker who simply acted out of character one time, then that is something else.

"I'd like to think that you are an honest, hard-working person that just became frustrated and saw an opportunity to vent your frustrations. If you were a bad guy, you would have asked for not just $10,000 but $100,000.

Also, you would have had a history of this behavior, but you don't. I also think that you would have never done such a thing had the doctor not fired you. It's not like you kidnapped and physically harmed the doctor, asking for ransom, which would be very serious. I really think that we have a situation that was the result of frustration, as opposed to plain greed and vindictiveness. Every one of us has said or done something out of anger, frustration or stress. Was your intent to cause the doctor to pay you the rest of his life to keep you quiet or was this only going to be a one-time payout brought on by the doctor's mistreatment of you? It was only going to be a one-time payout, wasn't it?"

Bribery Themes

A. Receiving bribes:

1. Contrast solicited versus non-solicited
2. Exaggerate the amount and frequency of behavior
3. Suggest the suspect solicited the bribe but never received the bribe
4. Gratuities and gifts are part of the business world; everyone is engaging in this behavior; suggest examples such as airline mileage, hotel points, gifts for bank deposits, rebates for purchasing a certain car, etc.
5. Intent was to punish an unethical or dishonest individual
6. Suggest suspect was conducting his own investigation into corruption
7. Blame a recent stressful event that occurred in the suspect's life, causing him to act out of character
8. Blame unusual family expenses such as medical bills, school tuition, marriage, divorce, vacation, etc.
9. Suggest the victim made the bribe seem normal as long as the

work was of good quality and performed in a timely manner

10. Blame alcohol for impairing the suspect's judgment

11. Blame the corrupt "system," suggesting certain industries or countries view this behavior as normal

12. If the suspect has been employed several years and has been involved in receiving bribes for only the last two years, contrast accepting money/gifts for just the last few years as opposed to his entire 18-year career – complimenting the suspect for being an outstanding employee for eighteen years

B. Paying bribes:

1. Suggest suspect's intent was to avoid expensive and unjust fines or expenses

2. Suggest the suspect believed this to be a normal way of doing business

3. Suggest the suspect was showing his appreciation for being treated properly

4. Suggest suspect was trying to save time or money for his employer

5. Suggest the suspect believed his employer had an unwritten policy to engage in the behavior

6. Suggest no one got hurt – in the case of paying a bribe to receive a government contract, the work performed or goods provided were of proper quality

7. Suggest situational as opposed to premeditated

8. Blame unfair competition – suggesting the suspect was simply trying to get a competitive edge

9. Exaggerate amount and frequency

10. Contrast one time versus several

11. Contrast offering a bribe versus paying a bribe

12. Blame judgment being impaired by stress, alcohol, drugs, anxiety

Example: Mike, a building inspector received $2,000 in cash from a contractor to overlook substandard electrical and plumbing building code violations.

"Mike, I am convinced that you did accept the $2,000 from the contractor but I think that he approached you and showed you that the work that he performed, despite not meeting building codes to the letter of the law, was still quality work that posed no safety concerns. The real question is whether or not you approached the contractor or if he approached you. It is even more important to know if you really believed that work performed posed no safety issues. You and I both know that sometimes people establishing specific electrical and plumbing codes have no clue about what is realistic. By that, I mean they have no idea about the cost savings by using alternate materials that work just as well. I'd like to think that you believed the electrical and plumbing work performed was quality work. The other issue is, did you approach the contractor or did he approach you to make the changes? If you were approaching every contractor trying to make hundreds of thousands of dollars then I would think you are taking advantage of your position as well as being dishonest. If on the other hand, you were just trying to give this one contractor a break so he could show a profit as opposed to a loss, then that's important to resolve.

"If you're basically an honest person and were simply doing a favor for this one contractor, we need to know that. Sometimes Mike, when a person is offered money during a time of need, an honest person can give in to temptation and make a mistake. If you combine a person's need with opportunity, a situation is perfect for anyone to do something out of character. Both of those ingredients were present in this situation. I think that is what happened here. On the other hand, some people are just plain greedy or dishonest, using their position to cheat and steal to maintain their high lifestyle. I don't think you received the money to buy drugs or gamble or take expensive vacations, did you? I think you were just doing a favor for a contractor and this was his way of showing his appreciation. No one got hurt! You probably had some bills that needed to get paid and this money helped you out, right? The question, Mike, is this, did you solicit the contractor or did he approach you?"

Burglary Themes

A. Blame the victim for:

1. Leaving doors or windows open
2. Failing to rekey the locks of a new house or apartment
3. Leaving the garage door open with valuables in sight
4. Leaving the house key where it was easily found – under welcome mat, on window ledge, on top of door molding, etc.
5. Not having sufficient outside lighting
6. Not having an alarm or not having the alarm activated
7. Having shrubbery around the house for the burglar to easily hide behind or trees too close to the house that a burglar could easily climb
8. Having a nice house in an affluent neighborhood
9. Not drawing the drapes, leaving valuables in open sight
10. Being on vacation and not taking the proper precautions, such as cutting the grass, shoveling the snow, stopping the mail or newspaper delivery, having lights on timers, leaving the car parked in the same spot for several days, etc.
11. Having insurance to cover the loss
12. Inflating the claim to take advantage of the suspect

B. Blame the suspect's adverse life circumstances:

1. Unemployed
2. Ex-convict
3. Poor education
4. Drug or alcohol dependency
5. Not having parents
6. Dysfunctional family environment
7. Peer pressure, i.e., hanging around with bad friends
8. Dishonorable military discharge resulting in difficulty obtaining a good job
9. Loss of a good-paying job, i.e., suggest the suspect could not change his lifestyle despite the loss of income
10. Bankruptcy
11. Spouse walking out, severely reducing suspect's income
12. Blame the influence of the suspect's parent's criminal behavior

C. Exaggerate the suspect's behavior:

1. Contrast stealing property versus raping or abducting the family
2. Breaking into one house versus several
3. Breaking into houses in this area as opposed to several other areas
4. Contrast taking money/property versus valuable research or business secrets
5. Contrast taking money/property versus setting the house/property on fire as an act of revenge
6. Suggest that the suspect could have taken irreplaceable personal family mementos versus taking property easily replaced
7. Suggest the intent was thrill and excitement versus hurting someone

D. Compliment the suspect for his choice of victim:

1. Suggest the victim has insurance
2. Suggest the victim could afford the loss
3. If the property is a seasonal or second home, contrast not taking property from a primary residence

E. Minimize the suspect's behavior:

1. No weapon was used
2. Contrast the level of sophistication (highly sophisticated versus impulsive)
3. Contrast one time versus several times
4. Contrast spur-of-the-moment versus premeditated
5. Contrast taking someone's life versus simply taking property
6. Contrast time periods that the burglaries occurred, such as one week versus one month, one year versus five years, five years versus all forty years as an adult
7. Suggest that the suspect was talked into this situation by an accomplice
8. Compliment the suspect for not taking personal or sentimental items
9. Compliment the suspect for not vandalizing the property
10. Compliment the suspect for not stealing all of the property

Theme example: Harry commits a burglary as a result of need for drugs.

"Harry, as strong-minded as you are to quit crack, before you even realized it you were trying it again – just one time. But as you and I both know, there is never just one time! You began using it on a more regular basis and before you even knew, the cost to get higher and higher exceeded your income. As sincere and well-intentioned as you were to quit, you just couldn't. There are some pretty respected, wealthy people who can afford all the help to quit their drug or alcohol addictions and they still fall back into bad habits, just like you. The only difference is that these people have more money than they know what to do with. You were not born with a silver spoon in your mouth. You had to struggle for everything in life. You just don't have the money or family support to help you shake your drug habit. So what do you do? You are forced to do something out of character to supplement your income to be able to buy the stuff.

"Understand this, what you did could happen to anyone, you are not unique or alone. We all struggle with our addictions or compulsions in life. Some people like me can't quit smoking cigarettes. I've tried hundreds of times. Once I even quit for a whole year. I then got cocky and thought I had it beat. What did I do after a year of no smokes? I had just one! You and I know what one means. I couldn't even imagine if it was crack that I was trying to shake! Some people can't stop drinking or stop their abusive physical or sexual behavior. But fortunately you didn't hurt anyone when you took that property from the house. That is so important. Our concern is this, did you simply take that property to help pay for the stuff (crack), a habit that you just can't stop or did you enter that house to harm the family living there?"

Child Physical Abuse/Neglect Themes

A. Physical abuse – blame the child's actions and behavior:
Recreating the victim's misbehavior or age may suggest the most appropriate themes.

1. Blame the child for not developing a normal sleep schedule
2. Blame the child's inability to eat normal diets resulting in additional time and expense
3. Blame repeated medical problems

4. Blame excessive crying
5. Blame the child for talking back
6. Blame the child for never showing suspect love, affection or attention
7. Blame the child for watching too much TV
8. Blame others for exaggerating the victim's misbehavior
9. Blame the child for not recognizing that he is potentially endangering himself (for example going into cabinets where cleaning chemicals are stored)
10. Blame adolescent misbehavior such as shoplifting, smoking, using drugs, vandalism, showing-off, etc.
11. Suggest the intent of the action was to correct a behavior as opposed to abuse
12. Contrast an isolated incident as opposed to a pattern of behavior
13. Suggest that the child constantly challenged the suspect's authority
14. Suggest the child threatened to run away
15. Suggest the child humiliated the suspect in the presence of others
16. Suggest the child played one parent or a relative against the other

B. Physical abuse – blame outside factors:

1. Alcohol or drugs, i.e., suggest alcohol or drugs can cause people to act out of character
2. Suggest the act was the result of bad judgment versus meanness
3. Suggest that nothing else worked
4. Stress, i.e., suggest that anyone can do or say things in the heat of an argument not due to meanness, but simply not thinking before acting
5. General chaos, i.e., blame the telephone constantly ringing, the doorbell ringing, the TV blasting, the kids crying, etc.

6. Job frustration, i.e., suggest overwhelming demands of the job causes uncharacteristic behavior

7. Twins or triplets were more than the suspect could handle

8. Blame unusual financial circumstances causing extreme pressure on the suspect

9. Blame the overwhelming demands from all of the other children

10. Blame family members for contradicting the suspect's rules or demands, thereby confusing the child's expectations

11. Blame spouse for constantly undermining the suspect's authority

12. Blame outside pressure – others suggesting the need for "tough love"

13. Blame the "bad" friends of the child for their negative influence

14. Blame uncontrolled anger

15. Blame the environment, "cabin fever," i.e., being in the house, in a car, or a hotel room too long

16. Blame sleep deprivation

17. Blame the suspect's personality, i.e., suggest that some people genetically are more aggressive

18. Blame a recent unusual event occurring in the suspect's life, i.e., death of spouse, child or relative, loss of job, recent diagnosis of serious illness, etc.

19. Blame improper training from hospital or parents

20. As a last resort, suggest the action was an accident and once the suspect admits committing the act, continue developing the above themes with the intent of obtaining the true intent, i.e., frustration, discipline, stress, etc.

Theme example: Paul has been physically abusive to his 14-year-old daughter Kimberly for the last six months. Kimberly is a freshman in high school.

"Paul, our investigation does indicate that you did strike and push

Kimberly into her bedroom door. The door broke and Kimberly sustained a broken wrist. You and I both know that this wasn't an accidental injury as you suggested. After talking to Kimberly, I think what happened was the result of her new girlfriends being a bad influence. Let me explain. Kimberly was recently arrested for shoplifting with these same girlfriends. She never got into trouble in grammar school, but in high school, it's a different story. Kim doesn't know much about these new girls because there are so many feeder schools sending kids to her high school. Many of these girls come from broken homes where there is no structure, no responsibility and no accountability. Unfortunately, some of these kids lack loving and caring parents like you, Paul.

"I think you told her to straighten out but she showed total disrespect by constantly talking back and challenging everything you said. I think your intent was to correct a problem but Kim just wouldn't listen. Had she listened, you wouldn't have pushed her into that door. She challenged your authority simply because she saw her new friends get away with it in their homes. She began to think they were cool and tried to emulate them. In other words, she chose the wrong role models. Paul, you're different, you're better than those parents. You have your daughter's well-being in mind. I can think back when my mom reprimanded me over something like this when I was young. She used to say, 'better you cry now than I cry later.' At the time I just didn't understand what she was saying. Now as a loving and caring parent, that phrase is as clear as day! You know what I mean. You could no longer communicate with Kim and took it to the next level. She got smart with you and you shoved her into the door which caused the wrist injury with the sole purpose of getting her attention. My concern is this, was this done to correct a problem or are you truly an abusive parent? You were just trying to get her attention, right?"

C. Physical abuse – minimize the seriousness or uniqueness of the act:

1. Suggest situational versus premeditated – suggest the incident arose spontaneously versus the suspect arranging the time and location for the confrontation
2. Blame the suspect's parents – suggest the suspect was aggressively reprimanded as a child and ultimately became a responsible loving parent as a result
3. Suggest that no weapon was used – contrast knife or gun versus only striking with hand
4. Suggest that the injuries are not permanent
5. Suggest that the injuries will heal themselves as opposed to requiring constant medical treatments
6. Contrast one incident versus several
7. Contrast death versus temporary or superficial injuries
8. Suggest the action was the result of "tough love," something the suspect believed to be appropriate

D. Physical abuse – non-family members:

1. Blame the family for not properly disciplining or supervising the victim
2. Blame the young age of the victim – suggesting misbehavior is expected or anticipated by parents but not by someone who does not have children
3. Blame alcohol, drugs or stress
4. Blame the family for not returning in a timely manner – the child was overtired
5. Blame the family for not giving their children love or affection – causing the victim to seek attention by misbehaving
6. Blame the family for not establishing and enforcing rules for their

children

7. Suggest that the suspect was not accustomed to dealing with more than one child at a time

8. Suggest the suspect's intent was to discipline or correct a problem – not to be abusive

9. Suggest frustration as a result of continuous bad behavior

10. Suggest one time versus several

11. Contrast impulse versus premeditated

12. Minimize the seriousness of the act

Theme example: Alice, a 32-year-old babysitter shakes and strikes Mary, an eight-month-old infant. The injuries resulted in partial brain damage.

"What I think happened, Alice, was something more as a result of stress and frustration as opposed to meanness or hatred. I don't think that you hated Mary at all as some people might speculate. In fact, I think that you really love infants; otherwise you wouldn't be caring for them. I truly believe that you are a very loving and caring person who would never think of harming or hurting any infant you were watching, let alone Mary! But sometimes a good person like you or me can reach a point in which we may do something we'd never consider in any other circumstance. That is what I think happened to you. We know that Mary was teething and her parents neglected to have pain relief medication for you so that you could help her discomfort. Had they done that, you wouldn't be here now.

"I think you simply became frustrated by Mary's constant crying despite all the care, attention and love you were giving her. I think that after not just minutes, but hours of constant crying and stress, you grabbed Mary, shook her, telling her to shut up. Did she? No! She cried even more. You got more frustrated seeing that your attention to her was not working. Without even thinking, you slapped Mary in the face hoping to shut her up. That brings up a very important question – did you strike her with an open hand or a closed fist? You see, if your hand was open, that tells me that it was done out of frustration. If, however, your hand was closed, then that tells me that you were acting out of meanness or hatred and your intent was not to stop Mary from crying, but to seriously harm her. Secondly, if Mary's parents had given her some pain medicine for her teething and she wasn't crying so much, would you still have done this? I'd like to think not.

"There is no doubt that you did shake her trying to get her to be quiet, but what I don't know, and this is very important, is whether or not you did this for a short time or for the entire evening. I think you shook her because she responded so strongly when you tried to get her to be quiet by slapping her. If you had taken Mary's life then we'd have a very serious problem on our hands. But Mary is alive, thank goodness. Let's put this unfortunate incident behind us. You weren't trying to kill Mary? You didn't act out of meanness! You are a loving person, right? I think this was simply done out of stress of the moment, wasn't it?"

D. Child neglect:

1. Insurance does not cover the needed procedure – leaving no option for proper care
2. The doctor's office is too far away
3. Blame being extremely fatigued and tired
4. Suggest no or little spousal support
5. Suggest suspect didn't think this was that serious
6. Suggest suspect was tired or under the influence of alcohol
7. Suggest suspect wanted to finish a project, i.e., reading a book, laundry
8. Suggest the suspect couldn't afford proper care – this was how

suspect was raised
9. Compliment the suspect for being a good parent
10. Contrast neglect with physical or sexual child abuse

Child Sexual Abuse Themes

This section will discuss themes relating to child sexual abuse for both family and non-family members. The age of the victim is a critical consideration in the selection of the appropriate themes. The younger the victim is, the more difficult it will be to blame the victim's physical appearance as an enticement to the suspect. Even though the suspect did find the very young victim attractive, he also realizes that society would deplore this motivation. Therefore, blaming the victim's appearance as a theme when the child is very young would not be the most appropriate approach, despite the fact it is probably, at least in part, a contributing factor to the suspect's behavior.

Additional themes must be developed that afford the suspect a more socially acceptable motive. In addition to blaming the victim's actions and behavior, outside factors could also be developed that would psychologically, but not legally, justify the suspect's behavior. Most suspects realize that this crime is viewed with great disdain by society. Therefore, allowing the suspect to save self-respect during his initial admission is crucial to the successful outcome of the interrogation.

Blame the victim's actions and behavior for leading the suspect on if the victim is age 12 or over. The selection of age 12 is somewhat subjective and is intended as a general guideline for the investigator. Common sense will dictate if there should be an adjustment to the theme selection if the victim is younger but physically very mature. If the victim is under age twelve, blaming outside factors for the suspect's behavior would probably be the most appropriate approach.

It must be remembered that the suspect, despite the victim's age, did find the victim to be attractive or an object to satisfy a sexual need. Therefore, the following themes focus on the suspect's age and whether or not the suspect is a family member. These themes are not mutually exclusive and may be interchanged to family or non-family members based upon the individual case facts and evidence.

A. Victim *over* age 12 (non-family suspect – teacher, counselor, minister, employer, etc.):

1. Blame the victim's physical appearance, i.e., being very attractive, physically developed/mature
2. Blame the victim's style of dress (such as wearing provocative attire) as suggesting their interest in sex
3. Blame the victim's actions, i.e., inviting the suspect into her house, voluntarily entering the suspect's car, sitting next to the suspect in a sexually suggestive manner, enticing or flirtatious behavior such as touching the suspect's arm or shoulder, etc.
4. Blame a deteriorating family or social life
5. Suggest alcohol or drugs caused the suspect to do something he would not normally do
6. Suggest stress the suspect was under at the time of the incident, i.e., divorce, separation, loss of job, serious illness, etc.
7. Suggest the suspect really cared for the victim and was showing love and affection
8. Minimize the nature of the sexual act or the length of time the event took place
9. Contrast whether or not the suspect is sorry or not for his actions

B. Victim *over* age 12 (family suspect – father, mother, uncle, etc.):

1. Blame alcohol or drugs
2. Blame the actions or behavior of the suspect's spouse, i.e., being verbally or physically abusive, diminishing sexual desires, loss of physical attractiveness, cheating, constant arguing, etc.
3. Suggest intent was to educate versus sexually abuse, i.e., to be instructed about sex by someone who really cares
4. Suggest the act was performed to show love and affection as opposed to sexual gratification
5. Suggest that no physical or verbal force was used
6. Blame religious beliefs, i.e., some individuals have justified having sex with their stepdaughter or natural daughter believing the victim was the suspect's spiritual wife
7. Blame the victim for being sexually aggressive, i.e., sexually attacking the suspect during a weak moment in his life
8. Blame the seductive clothing the victim was wearing
9. Contrast biological victim with that of non-biological
10. Minimize the duration of the act or the time period, days versus months or months versus years

Example: Paul is accused by Lisa, his 13-year-old stepdaughter, of having her perform oral sex on him between twenty and thirty times over the last year. Paul gives Lisa extra allowance money after each act.

"Paul, we know from talking to you today that you said that you would never do anything to harm Lisa or as you stated, 'to ruin her for her marriage.' I agree with you because I don't think that your intentions were to be sexually abusive. I think that this series of encounters of oral sex with Lisa started out very innocently. What I mean is that we know that your marriage is going through hard times. I think that you wanted it to work, but your wife was not willing to communicate or work things out. That stress caused you to drink a little more than normal. At a low point in your life, Lisa was talking to you and you realized that she was very mature for her age because she very clearly understood all of your problems. Compound the fact that she's not only mentally mature but also very attractive and physically mature. Her mother buys her revealing clothes that make her look like she's 25 years old. I also believe, Paul, that there was no force used, that she voluntarily consented. This situation sort of developed because of a series of individual circumstances occurring at one time. No one circumstance in and of itself would have caused this to happen but several elements converging at the same time caused you to do something that was totally out of character for you.

"I think what caused your initial sexual encounter with Lisa was the fact that your wife wasn't satisfying you sexually, let alone showing you any respect. Your increased alcohol use as well as Lisa's physical appearance and sexual maturity caused you to do something totally uncharacteristic. What is so important is that you didn't force her to do this. Another important consideration is the fact that she is not your biological daughter. It would be an entirely different story if she were your natural daughter. I think that you were simply looking for love and affection and really cared for Lisa. In fact, you didn't have sexual intercourse with her because you knew that would be wrong. You see, Paul, that tells me that you do have morals. Yes, the oral sex escalated to two or three dozen times but it was only over a year and not the entire thirteen years. That is what I think happened. I think this only lasted one year, if even that long. However, if it has been occurring over the last ten years and Lisa is mentally blocking it out of her mind, then I'd say that you were taking advantage of her. Paul, has this been going on for ten years or just over the last 12 months? I'd like to think it was only over the last 12 months. Am I correct?"

C. Victim *under* age 12 (family or non-family suspect):

    1. Blame alcohol or drugs

2. Blame the victim for unintentionally touching or sexually stimulating the suspect

3. Blame the parents for not properly supervising their child, i.e., allowing the child to sleep over, stay out late with older siblings, stay home alone, etc.

4. Blame the victim's parents for not providing love, affection or attention, i.e., suggesting the suspect's initial motivation was to provide love

5. Blame the Internet for "brainwashing" subscribers via child porn web sites, thereby normalizing this behavior

6. Blame the isolated area in which the suspect lives, i.e., not affording normal contact with the opposite sex

7. Blame the suspect's spouse for sexual neglect

8. Blame the victim's parents for neglecting to educate the victim about sexual behavior

9. Suggest that the suspect's behavior was motivated out of love versus purely sexual gratification

10. Suggest the victim was not the suspect's biological child

11. Suggest mutual consent

12. Suggest the suspect was abused as a child, i.e., stressing this as a learned behavior versus an aberrant behavior

13. Suggest the behavior is accepted in other cultures

14. Suggest that a significant recent stressful event occurred in the suspect's life, i.e., loss of job, divorce, separation, death of a loved one, etc.

15. Suggest that the suspect was sexually abused as a young child and cannot control or explain his behavior

16. Compliment the suspect for stopping when requested by the victim

17. Contrast the act lasting a long time versus a short time

18. Contrast one time versus several

19. Compliment the suspect for not using physical force

20. Minimize the act by contrasting something much more serious that the suspect could have done such as touching versus penetration

D. Juvenile sexual misconduct amongst siblings or friends:

1. Curiosity such as to see or compare body parts of the opposite or same sex
2. Experimentation such as to observe a reaction or to see what it was like
3. Influence of the Internet
4. Influence of TV or movies
5. Influence of other friends
6. Sex drive at young age being high
7. Boredom
8. Lack of adult supervision
9. Blame the parents for lack of supervision or neglect of proper sexual education
10. Minimize the nature of the sexual act or number of times committed

Theme example: Jane, a thirteen-year-old is kissed and sexually touched by Randy, her teenage youth minister.

"Randy, I believe that you did kiss and sexually touch Jane, but I'd like to think that is all that happened. Furthermore, you have been volunteering your time for just about one year now, which speaks highly of you. My other concern is whether or not this is the only time you made an inappropriate decision or whether or not you have been doing this to every young woman that you have instructed. I know that she came into your office last week wanting to talk to you when this thing happened. That is important because that tells me that you didn't arrange to meet her somewhere, which would suggest that you had planned this out for a long time. What it tells me by her coming into your office is that this was more situational than anything else.

"At the same time, kissing and touching are a whole lot different than having sexual intercourse. What really needs to be explained are a few questions – first, was this planned or situational? Second, was this just a kiss and touch or something more serious that she is afraid to admit? Third, and most importantly, was this the only time this has happened or have you done this to every young woman that you have instructed? Randy, let's put this behind us. Was this just an isolated situation of poor judgment? I'd like to think it was, wasn't it?"

Computer Misconduct Themes

A. Computer hacking:

1. Contrast computer theft as a form of trespassing as opposed to serious physical trespassing or as robbery or burglary
2. Contrast the suspect as being a thrill-seeking computer "geek" versus a serious offender
3. Contrast behavior as "social manipulation" or "social engineering" (as some computer thieves have described to minimize what they have done) with that of outright fraud
4. Contrast copying information without permission versus overt stealing
5. Contrast a terrorist act versus simply a personal challenge to beat the system
6. Contrast curiosity (to obtain financial records) versus elaborate identity theft
7. Contrast the suspect as being a juvenile expected to make

mistakes versus an adult who should have known better

8. Contrast extortion versus challenge, curiosity or boredom

9. Compliment the suspect for not disseminating or selling the sensitive information that was obtained

10. Compliment the suspect's superior computer intellect

11. Compliment the suspect for not causing physical injury or a threat to the public health or safety

12. Suggest the suspect was prompted or motivated by media coverage

13 Suggest the intent was to seek a weakness in the "system" versus trying to commit a serious crime

14. Suggest the suspect could have legally obtained the information but engaged in hacking to obtain the information in a more expeditious manner

15. Suggest the suspect's intent was just curiosity, to learn more about computer systems

16. Suggest hacking becomes an addictive behavior requiring professional help; compare to a disease such as alcoholism, workaholics, gambling, etc.

17. Blame the ease with which the act can be accomplished

18. Blame peer pressure

19. Blame the victim's poor security or controls

20. Blame the victim for improperly discarding sensitive information into dumpsters, failure to shred, not removing from information from discs, hard drives, etc

21. Blame the victim for prior mistreatment of the suspect

22. Minimize the suspect's level of planning or sophistication or do the opposite; particularly with individuals having a low self-esteem, compliment the suspect on his planning, sophistication and boldness

23. Minimize the damage created

B. Virus:

1. Suggest intent was a challenge
2. Minimize by suggesting suspect created an easily correctable virus
3. Minimize the frequency
4. Suggest suspect did not invent the virus but altered an existing virus, i.e., copycat
5. Minimize by suggesting the suspect did not affect a computer system used for national security or by an agency of the United States
6. Minimize the damage to a computer, computer system, network, information or data program
7. Blame others for challenging the suspect
8. Blame the victim for having poorly protected computers
9. Blame Internet chat rooms for glamorizing virus development
10. Blame Web sites for containing hacker and virus-writing tools
11. Blame boredom, free time or being laid off
12. Blame anti-virus software manufacturers for creating the challenge or not providing proper protection for the victims
13. Contrast bragging rights versus personal gain – describe others that have tried but failed to do what the suspect was able to accomplish
14. Contrast act with a more serious offense in which someone was physically assaulted, such as murder, rape, child molesting, etc.
15. Contrast attacking a specific operating system versus all operating systems – imply the suspect attacked a specific software manufacturer that appears to monopolize the industry with their products with the intent to get rich and destroy all competition
16. Contrast extortion as intent versus a lesser motive
17. Intent was to test anti-virus software – not knowing the problems this virus was going to create

18. Suggest everyone is doing this
19. Blame the media (TV, movies, newspapers, etc.) for glamorizing the activity

Example: John created a virus and infected a computer system via the Internet.

"John, our concern is whether or not this is an isolated occurrence or if you have developed hundreds of such viruses. We're also concerned about whether or not this was a random act or if you had a specific target in mind. The FAA had some glitches in their computer system, which, if it had proceeded to another level, would have resulted in providing misinformation to air traffic controllers. This could have conceivably resulted in the death of hundreds, if not thousands of innocent people!

"If the virus you created was designed to harm people then you're doing the right thing by saying nothing. On the other hand, if it was simply done as a challenge, to see if it could be done then that needs to be explained. At the same time, if this was an isolated incident as opposed to you doing this kind of thing on a regular basis, then that needs to be explained. John, you're an intelligent guy with some free time on your hands. You happen to be between jobs and sometimes the uncertainty of the future can cause a great deal of stress. You understand what I mean. Sometimes idle time can cause us to focus on things that we normally don't think about. I'm thinking this was simply your way of challenging your intelligence, to see if you could do it. While at the same time you were attempting to relieve some of the stress that you are under. But I don't know that for sure, which is why your explanation is so important. Was this done to harm people or simply done as a personal challenge combined with stress as a result of being without a job? You didn't want to harm anyone, did you John?"

Con Game Themes

1. Blame the victim's greed; suggest the victim knew his behavior was not 100% legitimate or appropriate
2. Blame the victim's gullibility making the crime easy to accomplish
3. Blame the unemployment or inadequate income of the suspect for initiating his actions or behavior
4. Blame the suspect's extravagant lifestyle as being out of control
5. Blame the difficult economy
6. Blame the ease with which the act could be accomplished
7. Minimize the frequency of the act
8. Minimize the dollar loss to the victim
9. Suggest the suspect did not physically harm the victim
10. Suggest intent was to provide for basic necessities
11. Suggest intent was a challenge, to see if the suspect could accomplish the act
12. Suggest this crime is not that uncommon
13. Suggest the offender did not destroy the victim's life, unlike identity theft
14. If the crime involves accomplices, minimize or exaggerate the level of the suspect's participation
15. If the crime involves accomplices, suggest that the suspect's level of involvement may be exaggerated by the other participants unless he explains his level of participation
16. Contrast the con artist as a person who does not threaten or harm people versus individuals that do, such as armed robbers, rapists, muggers, child sexual abusers, etc.

Example: An elderly couple received a quote of $2,000 to tuck-point their house. A man named Gary, who was driving through the neighborhood, observed the elderly couple looking at their house, which was in obvious need of repair. He stopped, was shown their written quote and told them that he could do the repair work for $250. He told them that he could do the job so cheaply because he was doing a similar job in the neighborhood and would probably have extra supplies when he finished. The couple paid the man $250 cash and never heard from him again.

"Gary, I think the reason that you took the money from the couple is because they were just being greedy and you knew that you could get away with it. But it didn't work out that way. The good thing is that you didn't hold a gun to their heads to force them to give you the money. They readily gave you the $250 because they thought they were taking advantage of you! They showed you a previous quote of $2,000 knowing good and well it was fair considering how much work was involved. You didn't deprive them of their life savings like someone else might have. Had you charged them $2,000 for the job then I would think that you're the kind of person that just doesn't care about people. Charging them only $250 tells me that you didn't want to cheat them out of their life savings like someone else might have done. In fact, you were teaching them an inexpensive lesson in life. The lesson: you get what you pay for. On the positive side, I'm sure that they will never allow this to happen again.

"Another concern, Gary, is whether or not this is the only homeowner in the neighborhood you did this to or whether or not there are other people who are ashamed to admit they have been taken advantage of by you. If you compare what you've done with what of all those corrupt executives at those large companies who stole employees' life savings from their pension funds, it's almost nothing. They ripped off millions of dollars from thousands of hard-working people. You only took $250! Another concern we have is whether or not this was the result of the fact you've been unemployed for months and simply acted out of desperation or is this your normal way of business? I'd like to think that it was an act of desperation, wasn't it?"

Counterfeiting/Forgery Themes

Technology has created an environment in which anyone with an inexpensive, high quality computer, scanner, printer and paper can easily alter or counterfeit money or documents. Professional counterfeiters engage in this crime using these and even more sophisticated methods.

A. Counterfeit/forgery themes:

1. Blame the suspect's inability to obtain a legitimate job
2. Blame unusual family expenses
3. Blame the technological ease of completing the act
4. Blame the government for over-taxing people, causing high inflation, high unemployment, etc.
5. Blame someone else's idea
6. Blame the lucrative offer to perform the act as being too tempting
7. Blame the Internet for providing the education and technology to accomplish the crime
8. Minimize the amount of money counterfeited, suggesting the suspect was not trying to maintain a lavish lifestyle
9. Contrast intent to destabilize a country's monetary system versus making a profit
10. Contrast the time frames in which the crime was committed, for example, one month versus one year; one year versus five years; etc.
11. Contrast one occasion versus several
12. Contrast forgery/counterfeiting versus a much more serious crime such as homicide
13. Contrast the victim as being a corporation as opposed to adversely impacting an individual
14. Suggest that the original intent was the challenge of the act, to see if it could be done

15. Suggest the suspect was threatened or blackmailed into committing the crime

16. Suggest it was done on a dare

17. Suggest no one was hurt as a result of the forgery/counterfeiting

18. Suggest the suspect's intent was to impress others with his intelligence or cleverness

19. Suggest the suspect was approached for a favor: to provide a document – birth or death certificate, social security card, driver's license, passport, visa, work permit, etc.

20. Suggest the counterfeiting/forgery was intended to help an individual or family obtain work or citizenship, hospitalization, education, etc.

Example: Alan has been counterfeiting $100 bills for the last year. He has had prior success counterfeiting money and is very knowledgeable about the process.

"Alan, we know that you have done this in the past and sometimes old habits are hard to break, especially when there appears to be no other option. What I mean is that we know that you have done time (in jail) for doing this in the past. We also know that sometimes a person wants to change but doesn't get the breaks in life that others do. It has to be difficult getting a decent job because of your past. This economy is really bad and employers have the opportunity to hire one out of a hundred people applying for one job. Who are they going to hire? They'll probably hire the youngest and most eager person for the job for the least amount of money and benefits. You just don't have a chance in the labor pool.

"Alan, I think that for these reasons, combined with the pressure to provide for your family, you went back to doing what you knew best, making money, literally. We know you've made 100's but are concerned if that is all you made or if the new 50's and 20's we're seeing were made by you as well. We know that you have been living in the area for the last five years and our concern is whether you have been doing this for the last five years or just for the last 12 months or so. If you have only been doing this for the last year then that tells us that you really did try to go straight. On the other hand, if you have been doing this since the day you got out (of prison) then that tells us that you're a true professional counterfeiter. Alan, have you been doing this for the last year or has it been from the very first day you got out (of prison)? It's only been for the last year, hasn't it?"

Credit Card Theft/Fraud Themes

These themes can also be modified for check fraud investigations

A. Primary themes:

1.   Blame the carelessness of the victim, i.e., leaving their credit card at a retail establishment/restaurant; leaving their purse or wallet out in the open; leaving their credit card bills in the mail box; not shredding or destroying receipts properly, etc.
2.   Blame the victim for readily providing his credit card number over the phone or Internet
3.   Blame the carelessness or poor security of the vendor which allowed others to access the victim's credit card information
4.   Blame the victim for not immediately reporting that the credit card was stolen
5.   Blame the suspect's difficult financial situation, i.e., unexpected medical bills, education expenses, rising insurance premiums, housing, etc.
6.   Blame peer pressure

7.   Blame technology and ease, i.e., blame the ease in purchasing an illegal item called a "skimmer," allowing the handler to scan a credit card, copy all of the information from the magnetic strip, interface the "skimmer" with a computer and print magnetic strips containing the victims information – these then can be attached to stolen or altered credit cards

8.   Minimize the dollar amount the suspect charged

9.   Minimize the number or times (frequency) the suspect used the credit card

10. Suggest the suspect found the credit card versus stealing it

11. Suggest the suspect was given the credit card

12. Suggest purchases were for essential items such as food, basic clothing, medicine, etc.

13. Suggest the victim could afford the loss, implying the victim will be issued credit

14. Suggest the suspect was influenced by alcohol or drugs

15. Contrast premeditated versus spontaneous

16. Contrast credit card fraud with a much more serious crime

17. Contrast fraudulently using a company credit card versus an individual's credit card

18. Compliment the suspect for not selling the credit card

19. Compliment the suspect for not stealing the victim's identity

20. Compliment the suspect for purchasing necessary items versus making cash advances

B. Use of company credit cards for unauthorized purchases:
The following themes may be developed when an employee denies making personal charges on his company credit card.

1.   Suggest intent was to reimburse the company at a later date but unusual expenses prevented the repayment

2.   Suggest the suspect did not have personal cash or credit available

to make the purchases
3. Suggest the suspect viewed the behavior as a perk for all the hard work the employer did not recognize
4. Suggest the company could afford the cost of the purchases
5. Blame the employer for failing to reimburse the suspect for previous company-related purchases
6. Blame the employer's poor controls
7. Contrast the charges the suspect made as insignificant in relation to the huge profits of the employer
8. Suggest the suspect was influenced by another employee, friend, family member, etc.
9. Suggest the employee did, at times, use the items purchased for work-related tasks
10. Minimize frequency or dollar amount

Example: Sally, a three-year employee, used her company credit card during the last eight months to purchase about $3,000 worth of computer software for her personal use.

"Sally, I think that one of the factors that allowed you to purchase software for your personal use on your company credit card was mainly due to the poor controls the company had in place. I think that if there had been better verification by accounting at the company you would have never purchased the software for yourself. In fact, I bet that you intended to repay the company for your first personal purchase but after a while, when the company didn't approach you for repayment, you just forgot about it. Then a short time later, you needed to buy some other software and since you were short money, you purchased it on the company credit card. As time passed, the company again failed to question you about the purchase. The more this happened, the easier it became to use the company credit card. It sure appeared to you that it was no big deal to them.

"Our investigation indicates that you have made a number of non-reimbursed personal purchases that you charged to the company credit card over the last several months. One of our concerns, however, is whether or not these personal purchases have just occurred in the last few months or if they have actually been going on for your entire three-year career here. If they have been going on for all three years then that tells me that you probably got the job with the intent of being dishonest. On the other hand, if this just started to happen in the last year, then that tells me that you are basically an honest person that used poor judgment, in part, due to the poor controls of the company.

"Another concern, Sally, is whether or not you purchased $3,000 or $33,000 or $133,000 worth of personal items. If you've made $133,000 worth of purchases then that would confirm to me that you are clearly a dishonest person. But if the purchases are only about $3,000 then that's an entirely different story. Certainly, $3,000 would not adversely impact the company's bottom line but $133,000 is a totally different story. Our concern is this, was this just something you started doing this year or have you been doing it for all three years of your employment? Are we only talking about $3,000 worth of purchases or are we talking well over $100,000 in purchases? I'm thinking it was only $3,000, wasn't it?"

Discriminatory Hiring/Firing Practice Themes

A. Hiring/promotion practices – when interrogating the offending manager or supervisor, blame or suggest:

1. Poor record keeping – suggesting it was difficult to verify relevant past information with respect to the victim
2. Accurate information such as support data, applicant flow, promotion data, etc. is difficult to maintain or obtain and requires

too much time to process

3. Hiring/promotion data was not provided by management or not provided in a timely manner
4. Following orders or suggestions of superiors
5. Complex or unrealistic government guidelines
6. Did not agree with the seemingly arbitrary government regulations
7. Intent was to comply not mislead
8. Owed a favor to hire/promote certain personnel
9. Believed other employers in the industry were doing the same thing
10. If it is believed that management is falsely claiming the hiring data was destroyed, during the interrogation suggest that some of the data in question may have been legitimately destroyed but certainly not all

B. Firing practices – blame or suggest:

1. Pressure from management
2. Fear of losing their job for not following a request to terminate certain individuals
3. Age discrimination
    a. Suggest the employer's philosophy is not to discriminate but to remain competitive
    b. Blame the industry for demanding youthful minds that develop youthful ideas
    c. Blame elderly employee for stubbornness or inability to accept change, i.e., working hours, work philosophy, etc.
    d. Blame elderly employee for resentfulness of new management
    e. Blame the elderly employee for taking advantage of every benefit the company offered

    f. Blame the elderly employee's bad or challenging attitude

    g. Blame the elderly employee's marginally appropriate physical appearance

4. Gender discrimination – suggest the employer believed a specific gender could perform the job better or was more suited for the work

5. Race discrimination – suggest the employer believed the workforce was being skewed too heavily toward certain minorities or non-minorities, therefore intent was to be fair versus discriminatory

6. Disability – suggest the employer felt uncomfortable with the employee's disability (physical or emotional)

7. Contrast illegal firing practices conducted over a short time period – one year versus a long time; a few years versus during the entire time the business was in operation

8. Minimize by suggesting the decision was not personal but rather a business-related necessity

9. Forgot to review government guidelines and employment records on a regular basis

10. Personality clash between employee and management

11. Employer did not approve of the employee's religion or nationality, felt threatened or was pressured by upper management

12. Suggest employer's perception was, "It's my business and I can do what I know is in the best interest for not only my business but for the employees."

13. Minimize the frequency of questionable terminations

14. Contrast motive for termination, i.e., discriminatory versus economics (to show a better bottom line profit)

15. Blame the terminated employee for exaggerating questionable hiring/firing practices of the employer

Example: Mr. Jones fires Gary, a 20-year employee, and replaces him with his younger son-in-law for half the salary and benefit costs.

"Mr. Jones, you do have the right to hire and fire staff but you also have to follow certain guidelines. The issue of proper cause is an important consideration. Gary has worked productively for you for the last 20 years. Our records indicate that he has not violated any company guidelines, nor is there any documentation of warnings in his personnel file. In fact, Gary provided us with his last performance appraisal, which was all very positive. By the way, a copy of that appraisal could not be found in Gary's personnel file. In interviewing Gary, a couple of things came to light with respect to his termination. Four years ago you instituted a 401(k) plan. Gary was terminated one week before he would have been fully vested. Twenty percent, a sizable amount, of his company match will return to the company. That seems unfair since Gary was not given any notice of termination and no cause for termination other than 'cutbacks.' Additionally, there has been no documentation of poor performance for Gary. Second, your records indicate that an 18-year-old individual was hired for 60% less salary, who is not eligible to receive any 401(k) matches for the first two years of employment. This termination appears totally discretionary, with no regard toward Gary's performance.

"However, Mr. Jones, sometimes employers make economic decisions with respect to hiring or firing without really thinking their decision through. That is what I'm trying to determine. If you simply made a poor decision by terminating Gary and replacing him with another individual, that can be corrected. Gary can be re-hired. If on the other hand, you made the decision based on a personal level such as Gary's race or religion, then that is entirely different. Was this simply an economic decision or was it actually a discriminatory action based on Gary's race or religion?"

Domestic Violence Themes

Domestic violence is generally the result of a combination of many factors. It is therefore incumbent on the interrogator to address several of the following themes during the interrogation. Based on prior knowledge, statements of witnesses or the victim, or information obtained during the interview with the suspect, the interrogator may become more selective with the following themes.

A. Blame the spouse (victim) for:

1. Not accepting financial household responsibility, i.e., paying bills in a timely manner; dealing with car/home repairs; living within the budget; etc.
2. Never showing appreciation
3. Always expecting the suspect to solve any and all problems
4. Not working outside the house
5. Working too much outside the house
6. Not taking care of the suspect's sexual needs
7. Not keeping a clean house
8. Not being a good role model for the children, i.e., using drugs, alcohol, obscene language, etc.
9. Never being home – always out with friends
10. Never having meals prepared on time
11. Not maintaining proper physical fitness
12. Not being responsive to the children's needs, i.e., helping with homework, obtaining normal preventative medical attention, having their clothes cleaned, having their bedrooms clean and organized, etc.
13. Not following orders, being too independent
14. Being emotionally abusive, i.e., demeaning spouse in the

presence of family, friends or children

15. Being physically abusive
16. Cheating
17. Being flirtatious with everyone of the opposite sex
18. Constant nagging; not knowing when to shut up
19. Always being negative – never saying anything positive
20. Spending too much money
21. Watching too much television
22. Siding too much with his/her family as opposed to suspect's family
23. Threatening to divorce or walk out of the relationship
24. Threatening to "steal" the children
25. Not communicating

B. Blame outside factors such as:

1. Blame stress, i.e., loss of job, constant bickering, unusual financial expenses, unruly children, etc.
2. Alcohol/Drugs
3. Friends, i.e., always telling you what to do – as an example, "Charlie, are you going to take that from your wife? I wouldn't if I were you."
4. Cabin fever, i.e., suggest that in the most successful relationships, an old adage sometimes proves correct, "Absence makes the heart grow fonder," suggesting in this situation the suspect and victim were together too much – a vacation or break was needed to maintain a healthy relationship
5. Gambling
6. Upbringing or culture
7. Blame suspect's or victim's aggressive personality
8. Blame medication or lack thereof by the suspect or victim
9. Blame stubbornness of both victim and suspect

10. Blame the victim for constantly comparing the suspect to others

Example: Vito is accused of punching his wife Tonya, in the face.

"Vito, we know that you struck your wife Tonya in the face, but what I'm concerned with is what caused this to happen? My experience has been that usually a combination of events occurs which may cause someone to do something he regrets, overreacting out of stress. We know that you're a good husband and a hard worker that accepts a great deal of responsibility, not only at work, but at home. However, in order for a marriage to work, it has to be a two-way street. Your wife has to do her share of the work and also accept responsibility. When that doesn't happen, a person can feel as though he is being taken advantage of and begins to get mad. It gets worse when you confront your wife on this matter and she appears not to care and starts yelling and belittling you.

"We know that both of you were drinking a little and sometimes alcohol makes us say and do things that we normally would never do. In addition to the argument, we know that you're having some financial problems. The credit cards are getting out of hand and the income just isn't going up like you had expected. Your friends are trying to give you advice but sometimes friends just don't understand and can give misleading advice. I think that it was a combination of all these unusual circumstances that caused you to strike Tonya. She just wouldn't shut up and kept belittling you. Vito, if she had just kept her mouth shut, this thing would have never happened. I don't think you meant to kill her or do anything really bad like that, did you? It was only to get her to shut her up, to listen to what you had to say, right?"

Drug Themes

A. Sale:

1. Blame the buyer for approaching the suspect
2. Blame a third party for asking the suspect to provide drugs
3. Blame the buyer for threatening to report the suspect if he did not provide drugs
4. Blame the suspect's past criminal record for preventing him from obtaining employment
5. Blame the poor economy for forcing the suspect to sell drugs to provide for his family
6. Blame family pressure and the need to provide consistent income
7. Minimize the frequency of selling, i.e., the number of times or number of months or years over which the sales have occurred
8. Minimize the type of drug being sold, i.e., marijuana versus cocaine; cocaine versus heroin; heroin versus LSD
9. Minimize the dollar amount of the sale
10. Describe the suspect as a small time dealer, supplementing his income versus a primary seller living exclusively off of his drug income
11. Contrast selling to adults versus children
12. Compliment the dealer for selling quality drugs versus the other dealers who are selling drugs that have been known to be harmful or even cause death
13. Suggest that the suspect was simply doing a favor by providing the drugs
14. Suggest it was too difficult to pass up such easy money
15. Suggest the suspect had no choice but to sell the drugs, i.e., if the customer didn't buy the drugs from the suspect, he would have purchased them elsewhere

B. Purchase or possession:

1. Blame the neighborhood by suggesting that everyone is doing this to one extent or another

2. Blame the buyer's life circumstances – the fact that he has no future, is in and out of jail, has no education and has no opportunity to secure a good job; drug use has become an escape for him – a needed part of his life

3. Blame peer pressure, i.e., doing a favor for someone

4. Blame stress, i.e., the expectations of others to get the drugs for them was too difficult to cope with

5. Blame the seller for approaching the suspect

6. Blame the seller for not charging the suspect for the drugs, i.e., providing a "free" sample; also suggesting that if the drugs were not free the suspect would never have accepted them

7. Blame addiction, much like alcohol or nicotine

8. Blame thrill and excitement, suggesting the suspect saw others purchasing the drugs and got caught up in the euphoria of the event

9. Suggest intent was for experimentation versus being addicted

10. Contrast own use versus selling to others

11. Contrast this as being a victimless crime, suggesting that no one was hurt

12. Contrast alcohol versus drug use; imply that drugs are legal in other societies and people have learned to control their use much like alcohol

13. Minimize the type of drug purchased

14. Minimize the frequency of purchases

C. Drug use during working hours:

Some of these themes may be modified to relate to non-working use of drugs.

1. Contrast the time of the day, suggesting that using drugs at the beginning of the day implies a drug problem, while just using them at the end of the shift indicates social use
2. Suggest intent of the drug use was for a good reason, i.e., improving job performance, improving school grades, improving athletic ability, to stay awake, to reduce stress, to lose weight, etc., versus a bad reason such as getting "high" to make it easier to commit a felony
3. Contrast using drugs during "working hours" (as bad) versus during lunch or break time
4. Contrast using drugs "on the job" versus outside the building (yet still on company premises)
5. Compliment the suspect for not missing an inordinate amount of work, suggesting the suspect is not addicted
6. Minimize the type or amount of drug used
7. Minimize the frequency, contrasting daily usage versus weekly, etc.
8. Blame peer pressure
9. Blame the seller for making it difficult for the suspect to quit because he always has drugs available
10. Blame the nature of the job, suggesting boredom, repetitiveness, stress, etc.

D. Developing dealer's names:

The suspect's primary concern in identifying the drug dealer is fear of retribution, either for himself, his family or close friends. Therefore, as a last resort, the promise of confidentiality may become necessary. It is important that the investigator adhere to such a promise if it is made.

1. Imply that the name of the seller is already known and that confirmation is necessary to validate the suspect's cooperation
2. Blame the seller for the suspect's present predicament

3. Suggest the seller is overcharging or taking advantage of the suspect

4. Suggest that someone will cooperate and divulge the dealer's name, implying the dealer will have doubts about everyone that he has sold drugs to

5. There are other methods to obtain names without the suspect actually "telling" the investigator the dealer's name. The suspect is advised that he does not have to "verbalize" the seller's name but is advised to simply write the name or names on a piece of paper. The suspect is advised that he has not technically "said" the names. The interrogator may even step out of the room for a few moments to give the suspect time to write the name or names on a sheet of paper. The implication is that the suspect has not "told" the investigator the name or names. Another option might be to have the suspect write down the dealer's initials (again suggesting he has not "told" the name to anyone).

6. Present a list of names of suspected dealers, some of which are fictitious, testing the suspect's credibility – the suspect is advised that the investigator will put his pen next to each name and to "cough" when a dealer's name is touched by the pen, suggesting the suspect did not "tell" the investigator the name

7. Suggest to the suspect that eventually someone will talk and the person that talks first is the one that will be the most credible, the one that people believe

8. If the suspect is reluctant to provide names, have the suspect provide a physical description of the person

9. As a last resort, suggest confidentiality, telling the suspect that his name will not be revealed to the dealer (do not suggest confidentiality if the promise cannot be fulfilled)

Theme example: Developing a drug dealer's name from Christopher.

"Christopher, this dealer doesn't care about you one bit; all he cares about is getting you or your family hooked on drugs and then charging you more and more money for the drugs. He is putting you in a position where eventually you'll do anything to pay for his drugs. It may be that you sell your watch, your wife's wedding ring, your kid's video games, but when all that stuff is gone what are you going to do? You are going to start stealing, maybe from your job, friends or family. When that money runs out and it will, the people that loved or trusted you the most will no longer care about you.

"Things will eventually get worse, like breaking into businesses, homes or even robbing people. Eventually someone is going to get hurt – maybe you, an innocent kid or an innocent bystander. Sooner or later, you'll be caught and the consequences facing you will be very serious. You and I both know that the dealer that started you down this dead-end road doesn't care one bit what happens to you. He will have others hooked just like you who will keep him in business. He'll be laughing at you for being so desperate that you would do anything to buy his stuff.

"He'll have other people buying from him that will keep him in business. Why protect someone who does not care about you? By telling us the right name, it will help us be sure we have the right person. Other people just like you have given us confidential information. I am not going to tell the person that you gave me his name, which would not resolve anything. (If such a promise is made, it must be kept.) But if you can confirm who it is, then that will tell us that you are not the main dealer. Are you the main dealer or just the buyer? I think you are just the buyer. How many people are you buying from, one or several? Who was the last person you bought from?"

Elder Abuse Themes

Whether or not the offender is a relative, friend or employee, the primary theme selection in elder abuse investigations should focus on blaming the victim's actions and behavior for causing the suspect's response, coupled with outside factors that may have adversely affected the suspect's judgment.

A. Blame the victim for:

1. Being unwilling to follow directions
2. Being cocky and arrogant
3. Constantly using vulgar language or racial slurs
4. Constantly demeaning the suspect
5. Pretending not to hear or acknowledge instructions, directives, conversations, etc.
6. Not taking required medication despite repeated requests
7. Being physically abusive, i.e., striking, spitting, scratching, etc.
8. Threatening to report the offender's actions, whether real or false
9. Childish behavior
10. Acting immaturely, suggesting the suspect could not believe an adult could be so irresponsible

B. Blame outside factors for adversely influencing the suspect's judgment, while at the same time, minimize the seriousness of the act:

1. Blame stress, suggesting the offender simply overreacted
2. Blame alcohol or drugs, suggesting the offender acted out of character
3. Blame peer pressure, implying others told the suspect not to

tolerate the victim's behavior

4. Blame the frustration that results from constantly having to repeat instructions

5. Minimize the frequency of the suspect's actions (one time versus several times)

6. Minimize the physical or verbal abuse by contrasting it with something much more serious that the suspect could have done

7. Minimize the duration of the act, contrasting a few seconds versus several minutes

8. Suggest that the suspect's intent was to correct a problem, even to protect the victim from harming themselves

9. Suggest the suspect's emotions overpowered his sense of logic

10. Suggest that the behavior of the offender was totally out of character

11. Contrast whether or not the suspect is indeed sorry for his actions versus someone who enjoys doing these kinds of things

Example: Jean, an employee at an assisted living facility, strikes and swears at Eleanore, an 87-year-old resident of the facility.

"Jean, I can understand why you lost your temper with Eleanore. I spoke to her and she appeared to be very aloof and almost sounded condescending when talking to me. She even asked me to repeat every question I asked her and that became very frustrating. I even began to wonder if she has a hearing impairment or is just doing that to be annoying. I know that you have just so much time to devote to each resident and that she requires a great deal of extra time just to accomplish the basics with her. I know that she is reluctant to take her medication and you have had arguments with her in the past over this. I also know that you have been at the facility for a good three months without a complaint. That tells me that you are a dedicated, hard-working employee.   I also know that this is a very demanding and challenging job, but by the same token, can be a very rewarding job. You have had such good rapport with all of the residents here that it just further confirms for me that you really mean well.

"I think her arrogant behavior, combined with her stubbornness and off-color comments simply got the best of you. By the fact that you did swear at her before you had contact with (struck) her tells me something. What it tells me is that you were warning her to take her medication when you swore. When she didn't take her medication after several requests, I think you just lost it and did this (struck her) just to get her attention. My concern is this. When you swore at her, was it for her benefit to take her medication or is this how you treat all residents? At the same time, and perhaps just as important, did you strike her because you enjoyed watching her reaction or were you acting out of frustration because she wouldn't take her medication? I think you just wanted her to take her medication, right?"

Employee Theft Themes

Most employees that steal money, merchandise or time, morally justify or excuse their behavior by adopting the belief that their employer, in some way, is being unfair to them. The most common attitude by the employee who steals is that he is being overworked and underpaid. This belief becomes the rule rather than the exception regarding the employee's perception of the employer. Other factors usually present themselves to further justify or rationalize the act of theft. One or more such outside factors may be: unexpected expenses, loss of income, poor security, mistreatment, stress, peer pressure, etc.

Additionally, the employee begins to believe that he is being viewed as an expense or liability rather than a valued asset. The employee becomes more and more frustrated and eventually justifies stealing to compensate for being overworked and underpaid by his employer. In his mind, the employee's actions are further warranted by his perception that he is the one being cheated. Certainly there are individuals who are dishonest and whose intent in getting the job is to steal from their employer. The following themes would still be highly effective for this individual as well because he also needs to couple his admission of guilt with a morally or socially acceptable excuse.

With this philosophy in mind, the interrogator must select the most appropriate themes listed below.

1. Blame the employer for not paying a fair wage
2. Blame unusual family expenses such as college tuition, mortgage, medical bills, etc. that caused such demands and pressure that the subject acted out of character
3. Blame the high cost of living
4. Compliment the employee for his good character, honesty and trustworthiness as demonstrated by
   a. Passing stringent pre-employment standards before being hired
   b. Having demonstrated their honesty over several years of employment
   c. Setting the standard for dedication
   d. Being responsible for keys, combinations, passes, etc.
   e. Being promoted on a regular basis
   f. Living within his means, providing for his family
   g. Having outstanding references
   h. Being involved in employment-related activities
   i. Being involved with noteworthy organizations
   j. Exhibiting good judgment skills
5. Blame the company for poor security or poor controls (thereby

affording the suspect an opportunity that he would never have sought out on his own)

   a. Lack of video surveillance cameras

   b. Lack of dual key entry

   c. No metal detectors

   d. No limits on employee access

   e. Lack of proper auditing/accounting procedures

6. Blame the employer for mistreating the employee, such as

   a. Not giving proper compensation for additional time worked

   b. Not giving proper credit for cost-saving ideas

   c. Not giving fair wage increases

   d. Not giving a bonus (or a fair bonus)

   e. Not treating the suspect as a "special" employee

   f. Not accepting the employee into the "clique"

   g. Taking advantage of the employee due to his age

   h. Giving the employee additional responsibilities without any additional pay

   i. Assigning the employee jobs and tasks that no one else would do or want

   j. Requiring the employee to be the first to arrive to work and the last to leave

   k. Having an unfair pension plan

   l. Having an unfair or even no health care plan

7. Blame the nature of the job in that the employee is constantly required to handle such valuables as cash, precious metals, financial securities, classified or proprietary information, drugs, etc., all of which bring their own temptations

8. Blame someone else for not doing his job

   a. Not properly locking the doors

   b. Not turning on the alarm system

   c. Leaving the safe open or the combination unsecured

   d. Not turning on the surveillance video-cameras

9. Suggest that most employees have taken something or done something of a similar nature
10. Exaggerate the amount that was stolen

Example: "Right now we're only talking about a small amount, it's not like we're talking about millions of dollars. I don't want anybody to think that you are the person responsible for all of the losses or shortages they've had in this area, which as I understand could be as much as $_____ (an exaggerated amount should be used here). It's important to get this matter resolved so people don't think that you are responsible for everything, which I don't think is the case. But I don't have a crystal ball, I'm not clairvoyant and don't know for sure. This is why I am talking to you, to find out exactly where you stand. If you did take everything that's missing then maybe you shouldn't tell me, but if that's not the case then let's get the truth on your side. Could you have taken as much as $_____? (Again present an exaggerated amount).

11. Exaggerate the frequency of the employee's activity
12. Suggest that the employee's intent was to help someone else
13. Contrast the employee's behavior as something that happened on the spur-of-the-moment versus something that was carefully premeditated and well planned
14. Contrast the theft as being committed for a "good" reason (such as food, bills or rent) versus a "bad" reason (drugs, gambling or extravagant spending)

Example: "One of the things that we have to look at very carefully and evaluate in a situation like this is why people do certain things. That can be a very important element to consider. Usually the honest person who makes a mistake like this has a really pressing problem that makes him desperate; maybe his family is in trouble, someone is sick, a car payment or car insurance has to be paid, money is needed for food or rent or some other very serious problem arises. Situations like this happen in life. If you're the kind of person who did this for a frivolous or bad reason, like drinking, or drugs or just to go out and have a good time, then that's a totally different situation. That kind of person doesn't care about anyone or anything. But I don't think you're that kind of person. I think you had a good reason, something that was really pressuring you and you acted out of character..."

15. Contrast just borrowing the money versus stealing the money

Example: "We've all had occasions when we've been short on cash and payday was still a few days away. Most everybody I know lives paycheck to paycheck. When you work with money, there is always that constant temptation, but you've probably always resisted it until this thing happened. What I think is it's going to be very important is to determine if this was just one of those times when you were short, desperately needed something, and simply took some money without permission. You probably had the intention of returning it at a later date. That can happen to anyone. I think someone noticed the money missing, confronted you and you were too embarrassed to mention what you did. You probably wanted to pay the money back but additional bills caused you to delay repayment. I'm guessing that is what happened. Isn't it?"

16. Overage theft theme

Example: "If we're only talking about taking some minor

overages and not all the money the company is missing then that is important to get clarified. It's hard to determine where an overage comes from and who it belongs to; it's basically extra money. It's not like we're talking about money that caused a loss or a shortage; the company got what it was supposed to get according to the tape or records. You probably balanced, found the overage, put it aside thinking maybe you'd be short the next day and when you weren't, this just happened. That's not the same as grabbing a handful of money from the cash register or vault and not caring if it caused a loss or not..."

17. One time theft versus many different instances

Example: "If this is the only time something like this happened, it's important to get that explained. But if this is the 100th time you've done something like this while you've been working here, that's an entirely different matter. We all make mistakes in life. Some people are dishonest, don't care about anyone, have a criminal mind and steal as much money as they can get away with. Then there's the honest person who works hard, puts up with all the hassles and pressures and then just makes one mistake in judgment and does something like this that is totally out of character. Do you see what I mean? This is why we have to get this thing explained, so that the whole truth is out in the open ...."

18. Original intent when beginning the job (to do good work or to steal)

Example: "There are basically two kinds of people who we deal with: those who come to work here with the idea in mind of ripping off the company whenever and however they can and those who come here to earn an honest living. My concern is which kind of person you are; the kind who from the very beginning intended to do things like this, or the kind of person who gave an honest day's work but just made a little mistake, didn't use good judgment and let the situation get the better of them..."

19. Imply the existence of incriminating evidence

Example: "As you know, when we investigate internal losses we have a variety of means available to determine what happened; we may use concealed cameras, undercover investigators, shopping services, information provided by customers, other employees and a variety of other procedures designed to determine whether or not an employee is involved in any wrongdoing. We have some of these things in place right now but I'm not going to tell you everything we already know about what happened. We know you're involved; I wouldn't be talking to you if we weren't sure that you did this. But now you have the opportunity to explain what caused this to happen. I don't think it was done out of greed or because you're just a dishonest person. I think you're like me, a basically honest person who made a mistake in judgment due to circumstances out of their control...."

Environmental Themes

A. Illegal Disposal:

1. Suggest that the cost to properly dispose of waste is just too expensive
2. Suggest that the suspect did not believe that the waste in question

was extremely hazardous

3. Suggest that the illegal waste was combined with legal waste, thereby reducing the concentration of hazardous material

4. Suggest that other countries do not have such rigid regulations and perhaps view our laws as unnecessary or overprotective

5. Suggest that this is basically a victimless crime, i.e., the highly restrictive regulations have been written to put money in the pockets of the politicians that have no knowledge of how to properly protect the environment

6. Suggest that there is confusion interpreting the laws

7. Suggest that the laws are always changing

8. Contrast illegal disposal a few times versus doing it every day

9. Minimize the disposed amount, i.e., 100 pounds versus 1,000 pounds; one truckload versus hundreds of truckloads; etc.

10. The disposal facility was too far away to make it financially feasible to drive there

11. The disposal facility was closed

12. The subject was just following orders

13. The subject was just doing it in an effort to keep his job

B. Improper Labeling:

1. Contrast improperly labeling once or twice versus dozens of times

2. Everyone else is doing it; it's a business necessity

3. Someone else's idea

4. Contrast labeling as opposed to not labeling at all

5. This has been going on so long, no one ever gave it a second thought

6. Suggest that the subject does not agree with the specific labeling differences

7. Suggest proper labels and paperwork were not readily available

8. Suggest that the labeling policy is unclear and confusing

9. Compliment the suspect for following labeling guidelines for several prior years and minimize this current mislabeling effort as due to difficult economic times
10. The subject was just following orders
11. The subject was doing what he had to so that he would not be fired

C. Improper Shipping:

1. The product that was shipped was not that dangerous
2. The product that was shipped was by a carrier with a great safety record
3. The product was not supposed to be shipped within densely populated areas
4. The distance that the product was shipped was not that great, i.e., within the state or within the country
5. The regulations are too excessive
6. The bureaucracy of the government made it too difficult to properly ship the material
7. Too much time was required to complete the paperwork, or the forms were not readily available
8. Minimize the frequency of improper shipping
9. The company's intent was to financially help the customer, i.e., keeping costs down
10. To maintain a competitive edge, i.e., in order to vie with the larger companies this had to be done

D. Illegal Dumping:

1. The company's intent was not to create an environmental hazard but rather to save money and provide jobs
2. Everyone else is doing it

3. Contrast placing waste in landfills versus in sensitive areas like lakes, streams, or other recreational areas

4. Minimize the suspect's disposal onto rural land versus densely populated urban areas

5. No one was killed or would have been killed if they came into contact with the waste

6. Suggest that this was done only a few times versus dozens of times

7. Suggest that the suspect was under a tremendous amount of stress, i.e., the job, financial, personal, etc.

8. Suggest that someone gave the suspect the idea

9. Suggest that the item dumped was in a secure container and would take years to degrade

10. Suggest that the waste discarded was an "eyesore"

11. Suggest that the subject was just following orders with little knowledge regarding the type of waste he was handling

12. Suggest that the subject was just doing what he had to in order to keep his job

E. Improper Handling, i.e., storing/using illegal products or materials that are not permitted:

1. Suggest that proper handling is too expensive and really not that necessary

2. Suggest that the handling of the materials in question was just temporary

3. Suggest that the suspect's intent was just to save money as opposed to an act of outright dishonesty

4. The decision to store/handle the material was based on convenience and safety and was not considered to be a hazard issue

5. Suggest that the subject was just following orders

6. Suggest that the subject feared losing his job if he did not comply
7. Contrast unintentional handling or storage of the material versus an intentional act
8. Minimize the frequency of the behavior
9. Emphasize that no one was injured or hurt
10. Reinforce the fact that precautions were taken to handle or store the items in a secure environment
11. Suggest that the subject's intent was to store the product for only a short time as opposed to a long time period
12. Suggest that the suspect believed he knew how to safely store or handle the material

F. No controls in place to prevent release of pollutants, i.e., air stacks, drain catches, etc:

1. Suggest that these controls are cost-prohibitive
2. Suggest that the company was planning to relocate to an updated new facility so that they would comply with all of the regulations
3. Suggest that the pollutants released were of a marginal concern
4. Suggest that pollutants were not released on a regular basis
5. Suggest that management has "unwritten" guidelines with respect to environmental compliance
6. Suggest that the suspect could not have engaged in this behavior a long time since the laws or requirements have just recently changed
7. Blame the government for not bringing these changes to the suspect's attention earlier
8. Suggest that other businesses are doing the same thing
9. Blame unfair competition
10. Suggest that the suspect failed to budget properly and therefore could not afford to implement proper environmental controls
11. Suggest that the suspect did not update controls for fear that the

new esthetics would lower the value of nearby homes

Theme example: Annette and her husband Frank, small-business owners, have been reported dumping lead-based waste onto government-owned forested land. The containers discovered are the same type that Annette and Frank use. Annette is being interrogated.

"Annette, our concern is not if you are putting your waste into the woods, but rather why and with what frequency. Let me explain what I mean. You and your husband have owned a small business in our community for the last twelve years. We've never received a complaint against you. Furthermore, you're trying to compete with the larger, more aggressive waste disposal companies. You only have so many resources. In fact, it is my understanding that Frank couldn't be here because he can't take time off away from the business. That even reinforces what I'm thinking, that you haven't been doing this for a long time and are being forced to do so simply to remain competitive. Also, you contained the waste in sealed 55-gallon drums. Most people that we talk to that have done things like this haven't gone to that much trouble to protect the environment. For that reason, I think you are concerned about the environment, and I'm beginning to think this is a financial issue and not one of recklessness or greed.

"I also know that the disposal facility is not necessarily convenient to get to and is not cheap. You have only so many trucks and when one is filled with waste and the disposal facility is closed, you have to make a decision. The truck needs to be used early the next day on another job. What do you do? You have to discard the waste, but where? Down the road from you is an area frequented by hardly anyone, right? You figure the site will not present an eyesore and the waste is secured in the drums anyway, which should provide protection to the environment. Am I right so far? Sure I am! What I think happened was that you either did what you had to do or go out of business, right? You're not a reckless business owner! I think it was purely economic, wasn't it Annette?"

Fish and Wildlife Themes

A. Taking game during a closed season:

1. Suggest that the game was for the suspect's own use, i.e., food, mounted display, or clothing from the hides
2. Suggest that the suspect did a favor for someone by providing them food
3. Suggest that the animal appeared injured and that the subject thought it would not survive
4. Suggest that it was a spur-of-the-moment decision
5. Suggest that the suspect mistook the game in question for a different animal
6. Suggest that the suspect hunted several seasons without taking game illegally and that this was just a one-time offense
7. Blame someone else for suggesting the idea
8. Blame the poor economy
9. Blame the fact that the suspect is unemployed and has limited income
10. Blame the suspect's employer for paying such low wages
11. Blame the fact that the hunting/fishing season is so short
12. Blame the animal's behavior, i.e., for coming onto suspect's property; becoming a nuisance by creating damage, eating flowers, disturbing the garden, scaring the children, etc.
13. Blame alcohol or drugs for clouding the subject's judgment
14. Contrast doing this during just one season versus doing it repeatedly over several years
15. Minimize the behavior by suggesting that the offense was

committed only days or weeks before or after the legal season

B. Illegal sale of game:

1. Suggest that the suspect was approached and gave people what they wanted
2. Suggest that the suspect felt sorry for the buyer
3. Suggest that the suspect gave the game to friends and was just given money to cover his expenses, i.e., gas, license fees, bait, ammunition, etc.
4. Suggest that the suspect was blackmailed or threatened by the buyer
5. Suggest that the suspect found the animal along the roadside
6. Contrast illegally selling game one time or during just one season versus doing it several times or over a period of several seasons
7. Blame the economy
8. Blame the demand and unbelievable amount of money offered for animal parts
9. Blame friends/family for pressuring the suspect to sell game
10. Minimize the suspect's behavior by suggesting that the animal was killed as a result of an accident

C. Guiding without a license or during closed season:

1. Blame the licensing agency for not providing enough licensed guides
2. Blame the fact that it is difficult to contact or find guides
3. Blame the sportsman for changing the type of game he originally wanted
4. Blame the license fee as being cost prohibitive
5. Suggest that the suspect is able to provide very good quality game for the hunters

6. Suggest that the money was just too hard to turn down
7. Suggest that the suspect was testing his ability to be a guide
8. Suggest that the suspect did a favor for someone and was paid to cover expenses
9. Compliment the suspect for having a commendable reputation
10. Contrast guiding without a license just to make a few extra dollars versus making tens of thousands of dollars
11. Minimize the frequency of the behavior

D. No business or fisheries license:

1. Blame the abundance of natural resources
2. Blame the economy, i.e., high unemployment, seasonal employment, jobs not available, expenses rising, etc.
3. Blame the high cost of obtaining the business license
4. Blame unusual living expenses, i.e., heating fuel, electric, etc.
5. Suggest that the suspect had a previous license or tax assessment, was not given one this season but had already incurred the expense of the equipment
6. Suggest that this situation started out as a joke, prank, or challenge
7. Suggest that game is plentiful and no one got hurt
8. Suggest that the suspect only made enough income to cover expenses and show a small profit
9. Suggest that the situation started out by someone else using the suspect's equipment
10. Suggest that people depended on the business for their livelihood

E. Fishing/hunting without a license:

1. Blame license centers for being closed, suggesting that the subject's intent was to purchase later

2. Blame license centers for being too far away
3. Blame the high price of the license fee
4. Blame the exorbitant cost of a "family" license
5. Blame the subject's excitement about the fishing/hunting; in his excitement he forgot to buy a license
6. Blame the suspect's friends for asking him to go fishing/hunting and this was an opportunity the suspect had been waiting for his whole life
7. Contrast fishing/hunting without a license as a one-time isolated event versus a long term pattern of behavior
8. Suggest that the subject's intent was not to fish/hunt the entire day, but rather just a few hours
9. Suggest that the suspect knew that he didn't have a license and therefore always released the fish
10. Suggest that the suspect's intent was to provide necessary food for his family and not just for sport

F. Spotting or shining:

An example would be taking game illegally at night using a light to disorientate the animal.

1. Suggest the fact that the suspect had a license but did not have the opportunity to hunt during the daytime
2. Blame the animal for approaching while the suspect was checking out the area for a future hunt
3. Blame peer pressure, suggesting that the suspect's friends talked him into doing it (spotting/shining)
4. Blame poor judgment, i.e., alcohol, stress, ego, etc.
5. Contrast the fact of doing it one time versus a pattern of behavior
6. Suggest that the suspect's intent was to provide food for his family
7. Suggest that game is plentiful

8. Suggest that the suspect disagrees in principal with the hunting restrictions and was acting according to his principles
9. Suggest that the suspect was frightened or startled by the animal

G. Using someone else's license:

1. Blame a friend for giving the suspect his license
2. Blame alcohol, i.e., impaired judgment
3. Suggest that the suspect was only fishing/hunting for one day
4. Suggest that the suspect could not afford licenses for his entire family so he was forced to use another's license
5. Suggest that the suspect intended to purchase a license later if he liked the hunting/fishing in the area
6. Suggest that the suspect intended to buy a license but did not have the opportunity to do so (the license center was closed or too far away)
7. Suggest that the true owner was not using his license
8. Suggest that the suspect could not afford a license or forgot to put his name into the lottery
9. Contrast that his intent was to provide food for his family versus selling the game for monetary gain
10. Contrast using someone else's license on one occasion versus using it several times

Theme example: Don shoots several deer out of season because they have become a nuisance eating the flowers and vegetables from his garden. He then begins to sell the meat to a neighborhood restaurant.

"Don, we know that you have taken deer out of season. We believe most were taken on your property. We also know that you have been selling the meat to the local restaurant/bar. The reason I'm talking to you today is to determine why this has happened. You've owned your cabin for seven years and we've never had a complaint like this against you before. I looked at your property and it's maintained very nicely. I haven't noticed any traps or baiting devices that would draw deer onto your property. Unfortunately, your property appears to be a natural pathway for deer to access water. That tells me that you probably got frustrated keeping them off your property. They can become less afraid of humans to the point where they not only become a nuisance but become challenging.

"If that's what happened here, where the deer became a nuisance disturbing your property and you just couldn't take it anymore, we need to know that. It's not like you baited or hunted the deer. They came onto your property. You probably tried to scare them by firing a few rounds, then after awhile, the deer became immune to the sound. What's the next step, to take one out? Does it stop there? No. It gets worse; more and more deer come. I think you did this to protect your property!

"What happened next? Your friend found out about your problem and offered you a few bucks for the meat. He tells you that he's having a hard time making ends meet running his restaurant/bar and you decide to do him a favor selling him some of the meat. Our concern, Don, is whether or not this started by you approaching your friend with a scheme to buy game for his restaurant. On the other hand, did your friend approach you to do him a favor and sell him some of the game? Don, did you approach your friend or did he approach you? After talking to you, I think he approached you, right?"

Hate Crime Themes

Hate crimes are criminal offenses committed against persons, property or society that are motivated, in whole or in part, by an offender's bias against an individual's race, religion, ethnic/national origin, gender, age, disability or sexual orientation. Examples of victimized groups include homosexuals, race/ethnicity, religious, homeless, elderly/handicapped and gender. The criminal act itself, whether homicide, arson, vandalism, terrorism, assault (verbal or physical), etc., is a violation of the law in itself. Therefore, theme selection may be chosen from those categories already mentioned in this chapter. Additionally, the following themes should be considered as the primary themes to address the specific motive – namely, the offender's bias or attitudes toward the specific group or individual.

A. Hate crimes against individuals:

1. Blame impaired judgment due to alcohol or drugs
2. Blame family upbringing, i.e., he was expressing the beliefs and attitudes he developed during his rearing
3. Blame peer pressure or hate gatherings for suggesting the act
4. Blame the suspect's misguided perceptions of the victim for causing him to act in a way that he believed was appropriate
5. Blame the liberal politicians for creating an unfair situation by "selling out" for the vote by enacting laws that favor the victimized individual's group
6. Blame the fact that the victim's clothing suggested a racial or religious bias
7. Blame the victim's behavior, i.e., being arrogant, cocky, antagonistic, confrontational, aggressive, etc.
8. Blame the government for promoting reverse discrimination

9. Blame the victim's actions (forcing his views, opinion or beliefs on the suspect, the suspect's children, relatives or friends) for provoking the suspect's response
10. Blame the victim for coming into the suspect's neighborhood for apparently no other reason than to offer a challenge
11. Blame the suspect's religious convictions, moral beliefs or lifestyle for creating the impetus for his actions
12. Blame the Internet for making the suspect's behavior appear to be "normal"
13. Blame the fact that the suspect's young age or immaturity caused him to engage in this behavior without thinking about his actions
14. Blame the suspect's employers for showing favoritism toward the victim's group
15. Blame the suspect's lack of contact or understanding of the victim, other than viewing the victim as stereotyped based on biased information
16. Blame the media for presenting biased television or radio shows that antagonized the suspect to such a point that he acted out of character
17. Suggest that the suspect committed the act simply to be accepted by his own group
18. Suggest that the suspect was inundated and influenced by the hate group's propaganda/literature
19. Blame the fact that in order to secure his own safety the suspect felt forced to act so as to demonstrate that he was in agreement with the hate group philosophy
20. Suggest that the investigator's intent is to correct the problem and possibly prevent retaliatory action
21. Suggest that the suspect believed he was exercising his right of freedom of speech/expression
22. Suggest that the suspect is now sorry for his action, particularly after observing the effects on the victim's family

23. Suggest that the suspect's intent was actually to help the victim(s) by acting in a less cruel manner than his more aggressive friends would have done
24. Contrast the fact that the suspect's behavior was an individual act versus being part of a large scale conspiracy
25. Describe the suspect's act as based on a situational or spur-of-the-moment decision versus a premeditated plan
26. Describe the suspect's intent as just an act against an individual or group versus trying to create community-wide unrest
27. Minimize the amount of force that was used; for example, contrast a verbal threat versus a physical act; contrast just displaying a weapon versus using the weapon
28. Minimize the frequency of the act – one time versus many times, just a few times versus hundreds of times, just this year versus doing it repeatedly over a number of years, etc.
29. Compliment the suspect for standing up for his rights/beliefs and not being hypocritical
30. Compliment the suspect for standing up for the "silent majority"
31. Suggest that the suspect only meant it as a joke
32. Suggest that the suspect simply wanted to see what the victim's reaction would be
33. Suggest that the suspect was simply trying to send a "message" that the victim was not welcome in the area

B. Hate crimes against property:

1. Minimize the extent of the property damage
2. Minimize the frequency of the behavior
3. Blame the victim for using his property as an obnoxious or offensive display of his lifestyle/behavior
4. Blame the victim's property as being an "eyesore" or blemishing a nice neighborhood or lowering property values

5. Blame peer pressure
6. Blame alcohol, drugs or stress for causing the suspect to act out of character
7. Blame the victim for moving into the suspect's neighborhood with the intent of being disruptive
8. Suggest that the suspect's intent was to "send a message," so that the victim would (leave, change their behavior, etc.) before more violent actions would occur
9. Contrast property damage versus causing injury to an individual
10. Contrast situational versus premeditated

Theme example: A physical assault against Howard, a homosexual, appears to be a hate crime.

"I think the reason this happened was because Howard engaged you in a conversation in the presence of your friends and your friends began making fun of you. You wanted to walk away but Howard's persistence in wanting to talk to you, combined with the taunting behavior of your friends that had been drinking earlier, caused you to act out of character. We know that you are basically a nonviolent person and you were not looking to hurt anyone. This was simply poor judgment on your part. We also know that you do not agree with Howard's alternative lifestyle and he should have recognized that as well. Did he? No. He began to talk back to you and before you knew it, you struck him. Our concern is this. Did you strike him because he was an aggressive gay with the intent of teaching him a lesson or were you really trying to kill him? I think this was a situational act brought on by peer pressure, alcohol, lifestyle disagreement and stress. You weren't trying to kill him, were you?"

Health Care Fraud Themes

These themes are applicable to violations involving physicians or medical clinics falsifying Medicare or Medicaid claims, as well as private insurance providers submitting falsified documents for medical procedures or services not performed, products not provided or patients not seen.

A. Blame the physician's fraudulent conduct on:

1. Unexpected personal expenses
2. A lifestyle that has spun out of control
3. Peer group activities, i.e., other physicians, clinics, pharmaceutical companies doing the same thing
4. An inadequate income
5. Excessive expenses related to maintaining a medical practice, i.e., malpractice insurance, hospital fees, cost of supplies, cost of employees' salaries and benefits, etc.
6. Excessive paperwork demands from medical insurance providers resulting in increased costs (hiring additional staff to handle the paper-work demands) and a reduction in the amount of time the physician can spend with his patients (with a corresponding reduction in income)
7. The reduction in the reimbursement fees allowed by medical insurance
8. The inability of the medical insurance provider to pay in a timely manner
9. The high cost of medical equipment
10. General job frustration, i.e., constantly being challenged by staff, patients or the insurance carriers
11. Gambling or drug addiction
12. The pressure from the clinic or hospital to increase revenues

13. The constant reduction in reimbursements for the same medical procedures which still require the same amount of time to perform
14. The industry "norm" of charging for services not performed
15. The excessive hours worked
16. Pressure from the family about the long hours worked and inadequate income
17. The insurance provider for having cheated the physician in the past
18. The carelessness of the insurance provider for paying him on invoices that were mistakenly submitted for procedures that were not performed or erroneously up-coded
19. The fact that it has been going on so long that it has became normal practice
20. The fact that this is a victimless crime – no one was hurt
21. The fact that the suspect was helping indigent patients who could not afford his services so he was just trying to recoup his lost income
22. The fact that the actual medical procedure performed was not covered under the insurance so a different medical procedure was submitted for reimbursement to financially assist the patient

B. Additional Themes:

1. Minimize the dollar amount involved
2. Minimize the frequency of the activity or the length of time over which the fraud was perpetrated
3. Contrast the patient soliciting the physician versus the physician initiating the activity
4. Contrast the minimal impact of the physician's actions and document alterations with the impact of a violent offender's behavior
5. Compliment the physician for performing life-saving medical

procedures which were previously not charged to the medical provider

6. As a last resort, suggest that the physician was investigating the flaws in the administrative procedure with the intent of reporting his findings

Dr. James Smith has worked for the local clinic for the last five years. His income increased 40% each year yet Dr. Smith is working 40% less time at the clinic. It is discovered that Dr. Smith has ordered prosthetics that patients haven't received. It is believed that he has received $50,000 from the prosthetic manufacturer for this fraud. Additionally, Dr. Smith has billed $100,000 for procedures that patients deny having received. It is estimated that Dr. Smith has received about $150,000 as a result of these fraudulent activities.

"Dr. Smith, it appears that you have profited from prosthetics not provided to patients and for medical procedures not performed. I understand that the work at the clinic is the type that oftentimes requires you to see the majority of your patients with the lowest billing return and the greatest amount of paperwork to complete. The point is that you are burning yourself out on all the care and paperwork required to earn what amounts to the lowest income of almost any physician with your skills and experience. When you accepted the job at the clinic, they glamorized the work and pay. None of your expectations materialized. You have loans from med school that need to be paid in addition to all of your other expenses associated with living. The question is what do you do to resolve this dilemma? Quit the clinic with no job prospects? No, you're forced to work within the system.

"What I mean by 'working within system' is to bill for procedures not performed because the system makes it easy, and quite frankly, everyone else is doing it. The system allows for it to happen by not having proper checks and balances in place to prevent the practice. Had the controls been in place, you wouldn't have done it. And by the way, I do mean 'practice,' because you're not the only doctor that has done something like this. In addition, the prosthetic manufacturer probably approached you and made it appear as simple as processing paper a few times a year to supplement your income. They benefited and you did, as well. No one was held up at gunpoint and you didn't do this for huge amounts of money nor on a regular basis. We know that you've padded bills by $150,000 or so over the last few years. That tells me that you've only been involved in about $50,000 per year or so, not $250,000 a year as one other physician I talked to was involved. This amount is nothing compared to some of those big executives scamming millions of dollars from their company profits, or worse yet their employee pension funds.

" The point, Jim, is that you didn't abuse the system to the point where it was done for blatant greed, but rather for need. You simply needed more income, but it was impossible to earn more because of how the insurance bureaucracy is set up. You didn't want to leave the clinic knowing that there were so many people in desperate need of your care!   I don't think that you are a dishonest person; in fact, I think you're a hard-working, dedicated physician wanting to provide the best medical treatment possible. But you need to live and pay your bills in order to provide medical treatment.

"Our concern, Jim, is this! Have you done this for only $50,000 a year or $150,000 total? Or, Jim, has it been $250,000 a year or $1,000,000 total? Has it been for $500,000 or a lot less?"

Homicide Themes

The primary motives for homicide include: passion, greed, envy, revenge, anger and the elimination of an eyewitness. Therefore, theme selection should attempt to focus on the specific motivation of the homicide that is under investigation.

1. Blame the victim for doing or saying something that provoked the incident, such as forcing the suspect into a homosexual act, reaching for a weapon, not following directives, acting in an arrogant manner, being physically or emotionally abusive, humiliating or constant bullying the suspect, etc.
2. Blame the effect of stress or other emotions that were caused by a devastating personal incident in the suspect's life, such as the loss of job, loss of a loved one, having to file for bankruptcy, a dishonorable military discharge, etc.
3. Blame the suspect's dysfunctional life, i.e., physically or sexually abusive upbringing, alcoholic parents or guardians, inconsistent or nonexistent discipline, lack of loving parents, etc.
4. Blame peer pressure
5. In sexually motivated homicides blame pornography for arousing the suspect
6. Blame the media for constantly reporting depressing news that exasperated the suspect's emotions, i.e., stress, anger, feelings of helplessness, etc.
7. Blame the media for constantly glamorizing homicides, thereby influencing the suspect to become a copycat offender
8. Blame alcohol or drugs for clouding the suspect's judgment
9. Blame cabin fever, suggesting that isolation amplified the suspect's emotions
10. Blame the suspect's aggression on prior training or activities, e.g., military, former gang member, living in a high-crime

neighborhood, self-defense training, etc.

11. Blame the emotion of uncontrolled anger for impairing the suspect's ability to think clearly

12. Blame hormonal influences, i.e., dramatic changes of estrogen or testosterone

13. Blame videogames for promoting or normalizing violent behavior

14. Suggest that the crime was situational, being at the wrong place at the wrong time versus something that was carefully premeditated

15. Contrast doing something like this one time versus many times

16. If the suspect is a serial offender, one option would be to select only one homicide the suspect committed, but the one with the most incriminating case evidence and information implicating the suspect. The suspect should only be interrogated on this one homicide. This tactic will serve to minimize the suspect's behavior by not advising him that he was involved in several homicides, particularly ones that were very gruesome. Once a confession is obtained, the suspect will perceive that he has won a moral victory, in that the investigator did not discover all of the other homicides. The interrogator should take a statement on the single homicide admission, and then interrogate the suspect on all of the other homicides, contrasting the total amount suspected with an artificially inflated number. Since the suspect has already made a homicide admission and has observed no shock or disgust from the investigator, it now becomes easier for the suspect to reveal the other homicides.

17. If the suspect has committed a series of homicides during the last few years, contrast these last two or three years with his entire life. It may be suggested to the suspect that he has led an exemplary life for 30 years and his behavior over these last few years is more of an aberration, indicating that something

happened in his life that caused him to begin acting totally out of character. Imply that your intent is to determine the cause behind the crime as opposed to soliciting an admission of guilt. To this end, suggest possible motivators which may have contributed to the suspect's criminal behavior such as: loss of a loved one, loss of a job, the use of alcohol or drugs, etc.

18. If the suspect is a serial killer of females, blame women in general for their actions or behavior, i.e., demeaning the suspect, mistreatment, abusive behavior, etc. Blame in general the treatment of females toward the suspect as a factor influencing his behavior toward women. These females may include the suspect's mother, sisters, fellow students, coworkers and past females whom he dated or those who rejected him in some way. Suggest that the suspect's behavior was not directed specifically toward the victim, but at all the other females that misunderstood or abused the suspect. Additionally, introduce some specific stressor such as loss of job, death of loved one, divorce, loss of custody rights, etc. that may have prompted the criminal act.

19. As a last resort tactic, consider contrasting the murder as a premeditated act versus a spontaneous act (this theme may reduce the suspect's intent and therefore the related sentencing so it should be used cautiously). As an example, if the case facts indicate that a suspect hid for fifteen minutes waiting for an opportunity to shoot the victim, it could be suggested that the crime was more situational as opposed to planned out for a long period of time. It could be suggested that one of the primary concerns is to determine whether this act was planned out weeks ahead of time or was the result of something that had just erupted that night, perhaps just a few hours before the event; the implication is an act that was very nearly spontaneous versus one that was carefully planned and premeditated. When the suspect admits that the crime occurred because of something that had just

happened that night, he may be asked how long he waited for the victim with the gun – "a long time or just a short time?" If the suspect responds, "Just a short time, only fifteen minutes," the suspect has acknowledged premeditation.

20. Another "last resort tactic" would be to suggest that the killing was an accident. This suggestion could certainly give the suspect a defense so the investigator should only use this tactic with that understanding in mind when other approaches have proven to be unsuccessful. The investigator's intent with this last resort tactic is to discredit the suspect's prior denials of having anything to do with the victim's death.

When the homicide is motivated by euthanasia or mercy killing, the following are themes to be considered:

1. Suggest that the victim made a request to terminate his life
2. Suggest that the victim's family made a request to terminate the victim's life
3. Suggest that the suspect's intent was to relieve the victim from the extreme physical discomfort or pain that they were experiencing
4. Blame the medical profession for not providing the victim with the proper physical or emotional support to deal with their situation
5. Blame the suspect's behavior on the stress of the job, i.e., constantly working in a depressing environment
6. Suggest that the victim's health was thought to be terminal anyway
7. Suggest that the suspect's intent was an expression of his compassion for the victim – an effort to help the victim who was in a desperate situation
8. Suggest that the suspect provided the means to the victim to commit the act, but that the victim carried out the act

9. Suggest that the suspect's action is not unique, i.e., he is not the only person that has done something like this

10. Suggest to the suspect that there are books written on the subject matter and even Internet articles implying the humanity of the act

11. Suggest that the victim was unable to pay for proper treatment

12. Minimize the number of times that the suspect has engaged in this type of behavior

13. Describe the crime as a merciful act versus a cold-blooded killing

14. Praise the suspect for doing what most people would have done had they known all of the circumstances surrounding the victim's situation

15. Compliment the suspect's method as being humane and painless

Theme example: Sam kills Laura, his wife of five years. There are no children involved. Sam recently took a $250,000 life insurance policy on Laura. Sam has been seen socializing on several occasions with Laura's friend Debbie. Laura's body was discovered in a nearby lake, the cause of death, strangulation. She was not sexually abused and was wearing her diamond ring and ruby bracelet.

"Sam, our investigation indicates that you did cause the death of your wife, Laura. What I think happened was the result of an argument that got out of control. I don't think you married Laura with the intention of doing something like this. I think you really loved each other. I also think that your relationship began to change or deteriorate over the years. Laura really wanted kids, thinking that children would help the marriage. You knew children wouldn't help, but in fact would become more of a problem to the marriage. Also, you were hesitant because you didn't want them brought up in a family that you believed would shortly end up in divorce. You were acting out of logic and common sense; Laura was acting totally irrationally. I'll bet your talks with Laura always ended with an argument about having children. Sooner or later she's going to challenge your true motives for not wanting children. She begins to figure out that you really want a divorce. You also realize that when she's losing an argument she challenges you by suggesting that she would make the divorce as difficult as possible for you; she even threatens to make your life miserable, a total nightmare!

"Sam, if Laura had not threatened you as she did, you wouldn't be here right now. We know that you're a decent, hard-working guy. If you had used poison, or a gun, or a knife to take Laura's life, then I'd say you were planning this for a long time, that you were a bad person. But the results indicated that she was choked. That tells me that this was a situational thing that was the end result of a very heated argument. If Laura had only worked with you and acted more rationally, you wouldn't be here right now. Sam, I'm thinking that this was the result of a heated argument, wasn't it? This wasn't something so sinister that you married her with the intent of collecting the insurance money, was it? Sam, this was more spontaneous, wasn't it?"

Identity Theft Themes

When an individual's financial documents – credit cards, bank records or personal identification documents such as a driver's license or Social Security card are stolen and used to commit a felony, identity theft has been committed. This crime may be perpetrated simply by someone finding a wallet and taking advantage of an opportunity or by someone who is carefully searching the Internet for information that they can use to perpetrate criminal acts via identity theft.

1. Blame retailers for carelessly displaying credit card numbers, expiration dates and names on receipts or internal records
2. Blame the victim for leaving his mail in his mailbox overnight or

over the weekend, thereby presenting an opportunity to a suspect

3. Blame the victim for not taking his mail to the U.S. Postal Service or placing it in a U.S. Postal collection box, but carelessly leaving it in his mailbox

4. Blame the U.S. Postal Service for misdirecting the victim's mail to the suspect

5. Blame the victim for providing sensitive information over the telephone

6. Blame the victim for noting sensitive information on his personal checks

7. Blame the general carelessness of the victim, i.e., discarding a computer without removing the hard drive, not paying attention to others eavesdropping, etc.

8. Blame the victim for discarding store receipts containing sensitive information

9. Blame the victim for not shredding sensitive documents

10. Blame the victim for not changing passwords on a regular basis or leaving passwords in an unsecured place

11. Blame the victim for not securing or carelessly using their PIN (personal identification number)

12. Blame the lack of security on the Internet, i.e., a browser that does not encrypt or scramble information

13. Blame the overall ease with which the act could be accomplished

14. Blame another individual for showing the suspect how easily this could be accomplished

15. Blame financial institutions for mailing sensitive information

16. Blame the "system" for having poor controls

17. Blame the victim's actions or behavior toward the suspect, i.e., verbal or physical abuse, threats, lies, etc., for provoking the suspect's behavior

18. Blame the economy for not providing decent paying jobs, forcing the suspect to engage in this behavior

19. Blame the suspect's overwhelming financial obligations
20. Blame the Social Security Administration or Department of Motor Vehicle licensing for carelessness and making personal data easily available
21. Blame the carelessness of the credit bureaus for making it easy for anyone to obtain confidential information
22. Blame the accounting/payroll firm the victim uses for carelessness
23. Blame the victim's employer for carelessness, i.e., giving information over the phone, not securing sensitive information, etc.
24. Blame the suspect's poor judgment or the stress that they were under, causing them to act out of character
25. Contrast the suspect's intent for needing the identity for a passport versus using it to commit financial crimes, such as posing as the victim to steal his financial assets
26. Minimize the damage that the victim will incur, suggesting that he will be issued new credit cards, his credit will not be adversely affected, etc.
27. Minimize the suspect's behavior by contrasting "just taking paper" versus taking someone's life
28. Minimize the frequency of his behavior
29. Suggest that the suspect was doing research into stealing identities
30. Suggest that the crime started out as just a challenge – just trying to see if it could be done
31. Suggest that the victim could afford the loss
32. Suggest the suspect was going to use the information for personal use versus selling the information to others
33. Compliment the suspect for being bold, clever and daring

Theme example: Kevin, a bank employee, steals the confidential information of Casey, a bank customer. He uses this information to make about $20,000 worth of purchases.

"Kevin, there is no doubt that you made purchases under Casey's identity. I think the reason that this happened was due to the bank's lack of proper security controls and your basic need for a little more income. One of our primary concerns is whether or not you were the only person that used Casey's information or if you sold this information to other individuals. The store where you made the purchases obviously doesn't care who is making the purchase, all they care about is making a sale. Casey's credit will be corrected and I'm sure that he won't be responsible for the purchases that you made. It would be different if he had to pay for everything. It's not like you used a gun to stick him up, or broke into the bank's computer system or rummaged through Casey's garbage. The reason that you took the information was because it was easy to do. In fact, what you did was to bring to the bank's attention the flaws in their system. You, in essence, identified a problem before others may have done something much worse. I don't think that you got the job with the intention of doing something like this. I know things are tough for you right now. The bank isn't paying you a lot of money; in fact, you're not making a whole lot more than minimum wage if you factor in all the hours you're working. When you put these facts together – income, need, the bank not recognizing you as a valued employee, the flaws in the system, I can readily see that this was something waiting to happen.

"Kevin, our concern is, were you selling this information to other people or were you just using it for yourself? Another concern is if we go into the system, are we going to find hundreds of other identities stolen? Kevin, I think you took Casey's personal information not to sell or to ruin the guy, but simply to buy some things for yourself. I also think that the bank's lack of controls made this too tempting. Have you sold Casey's information or was this just for your personal use?"

Indecent Exposure Themes

1. Blame alcohol or drugs for clouding the suspect's judgment, which subsequently resulted in acting in a manner that was totally uncharacteristic for him

2. Blame the victim's taunting or flirtatious behavior for leading the suspect on

3. Blame the effect that the stress from a recent traumatic event (such as loss of job, divorce, recent death of loved one, etc.) had on the suspect

4. Suggest that the act was just an innocent dare as a result of peer pressure

5. Suggest that the suspect's intent was to engage in this behavior as just a joke

6. Suggest that the suspect was relieving himself and simply decided to see how the victim would react

7. Suggest that the suspect was simply acting out an unfulfilled fantasy

8. Suggest that the suspect's behavior was just the result of a spur-of-the-moment decision versus a carefully premeditated act

9. Contrast engaging in this type of behavior on one, isolated occasion versus doing it all of the time

10. Minimize the behavior by contrasting the suspect's motives between doing it just for the intent to shock or stimulate a reaction versus attempting to assault the victim

11. Minimize the act by pointing out that the suspect did not touch or hurt anyone

12. Minimize the act by contrasting a situation in which the suspect exposed himself to an adult versus doing something like this in front of a young child

13. If the suspect is a youngster under the age of 15, contrast the seriousness of the situation if it involved an adult who should

have known better versus the poor decision of a juvenile

14. Minimize the suspect's behavior by contrasting the location of incident; for example, doing it from inside his car versus confronting the victim outside the vehicle; standing on his own property versus following the person to a remote location; doing it in a public area versus doing it on school grounds

15. Minimize the suspect's intent by pointing out that he did this in the middle of the day when lots of people are around versus doing it at night in an isolated area

Example: Albert, a 55-year-old father and husband was accused of exposing himself to a 17-year-old female car wash attendant/cashier while seated in his car.

"Albert, there is no doubt that you did expose yourself to Mary at the car wash, but I have to ask myself, why did you do this? I really don't think that your intentions were to force her to engage in sexual intercourse. I think your intent was to simply see a reaction from her. We know that you have been to the car wash on previous occasions and had harmless conversations with Mary. I think that you simply misinterpreted her flirtatious behavior and without thinking, acted out a fantasy. I'd like to believe that you just wanted to see her reaction. Mary told us that when she screamed, you immediately covered yourself up. Had you been a molester or pervert, you wouldn't have covered up, but would have taken it to the next level, talking dirty, demanding sex and things like that. But you didn't, you acted responsibly by covering yourself and leaving. We know that you're a good family man, which is also very important. That makes me believe that this was an isolated incident. By saying nothing, you are letting people think that you are doing things like this all the time. I don't think that's the case.

"My concern, Albert, is whether or not this was the first time you did this at the car wash or whether or not you have done this on previous occasions and the employees are afraid to report you. If this was only a fantasy and the first time you did this at the car wash, we need to know that. Was this done with the intent to have sex with Mary or simply as a joke to see a reaction? I'm thinking it was the first time you did this at the car wash and was intended as a harmless joke. Right?"

Insurance Fraud Themes

A. Homeowner's insurance fraud:

1.   Blame the high premiums or continually escalating premiums for causing the suspect to act in a manner so as to recoup some of his costs

2.   Blame the insurance carrier for having poor controls, for failing to investigate past legitimate claims, thereby giving the suspect the idea of submitting an inflated or exaggerated claim

3.   Blame someone else for giving the suspect this idea

4.   Blame the stress that the suspect was under from unusual life circumstances, i.e., loss of job, bankruptcy, college expenses, need for a vehicle to get to and from work, etc., for causing the suspect to act out of character and make a poor decision

5.   Blame the insurance company for failing to fully compensate the suspect on a prior claim

6.   Suggest that the insurance company could afford the loss, and in fact, has calculated the existence of such claims in determining their premium rates

7.   Suggest that the suspect's intent was simply to cover the deductible versus falsifying the entire claim for profit

8.   Suggest that this was a one-time incident and that subject only did it because he heard that all of his neighbors were doing the same

thing (inflating the extent of damage from the recent flood, hurricane, fire, etc)

9. Minimize the suspect's behavior by contrasting what he did with a violent crime such as armed robbery, burglary, kidnapping, rape, etc.

10. Minimize the psychological culpability of the suspect by pointing out how he has paid insurance premiums for several years without ever submitting a claim

11. Minimize the dollar loss

Theme example: Sonya falsely reports that she lost her $3,500 diamond bracelet. A local pawnshop reports that they gave an individual that reportedly looks very similar to Sonya $1,000 for a similar type of diamond bracelet.

"Sonya, we know that you sold your bracelet for $1,000 and submitted a claim stating that you lost your bracelet. How could this be true? Well, what I'm suggesting is that it is possible that you really did lose your bracelet, filed a claim, and then found it! If this claim was filed with no intentions to defraud the insurance company, we need to know that. On the other hand, if it was done to defraud the insurance company, then that tells me that you are a basically dishonest person. But I don't think that you are. I'm thinking that you're an opportunist, a good person that was put into a situation that was just too hard to pass up. It's kind of like finding a $100 bill when you really need the money. You see someone very well dressed, wearing all kinds of jewelry, driving a Mercedes and they are asking, 'I think I lost a $100 bill; did anyone find it?' You found the bill. Are you really going to give that person the bill? Probably not! That person is just like a rich insurance company, right? Do they really need money? No. But I'll bet if it was a different person that lost the money, a person that was really down and out and lost their life savings of a $100 bill, you'd have returned it, right? Sonya was this just an opportune situation or were you trying to defraud the insurance company? This was just an opportunistic act, right?"

B. Auto insurance fraud:
Examples would include fraudulent theft, fire or other hazard damage.

1. Suggest that the suspect was victimized by purchasing a vehicle that was unreliable and costly to operate
2. Suggest that the suspect was lied to regarding the condition of the vehicle when he purchased it
3. Suggest that the suspect was influenced by others to burn or fake the theft of his vehicle
4. Suggest that the suspect's intent was to break even versus trying to make a profit
5. Suggest that the suspect's decision to perpetrate this act was made on impulse due to the stress he was under or the fact that his judgment was clouded by alcohol, as opposed to maliciously planning it out over a long period of time
6. Blame the high cost of insurance, particularly the fact that the premiums were much higher than he had been led to believe before purchasing the vehicle
7. Blame unusual family expenses
8. Blame his loss of job or a reduction of income, creating a desperate financial situation
9. Blame the suspect's employer for requiring the suspect to own the type of vehicle that he could not afford
10. Compliment the suspect for not hurting anyone, comparing insurance fraud with a very serious crime in which an individual was severely hurt

Theme example: Victor reports his car stolen. Victor's car was discovered two weeks later showing no signs of forced entry and the interior had been set on fire. The suspect was three months behind in payments. It was discovered from the local repair shop that Victor had recently spent hundreds of dollars on repairs and was recently informed that the car needed a new transmission.

"Victor, we know that you faked the theft of your car. We think that the reason you did this was not to profit by it but just to break even. We know that the car required repeated and extensive repairs and was not as reliable as you had expected. You purchased the car used just eight months ago and I'm thinking the person that sold you the car took advantage of you. He knew the car was going to need extensive repairs. Did he tell you? No. He wanted to get rid of a lemon and cheat a good person. You bought the car in good faith thinking that it was going to be reliable. You're different from this dishonest guy. You're basically an honest person. You didn't cheat a hard-working person by selling him a lemon. You just wanted to break even and got rid of the car so that no one else would be cheated. For that, I compliment you.

"However, Victor, our concern is to determine whether or not you simply got tired and bored with the car and didn't want to take the time and effort it would take to sell it. On the other hand, if you simply got so frustrated with all the money you had to keep pouring into it and all the work you missed because the car was always in the shop that you made a mistake in judgment and decided to fake a theft. I know you're not made of money. The car became a nightmare; just when it was repaired, something else broke. I think that you simply wanted to break even and you certainly didn't want to cheat anyone by selling them such a terrible car. I don't think you were trying to make money on the claim; you were simply trying to break even, weren't you Victor?"

C. Personal liability fraud:
Acts of negligence – slip and fall on personal or business property, auto

accident, etc.

1. Suggest that the "victim" (either a private residence or business) could afford the claim since the insurance carrier will pay the damages
2. Suggest that the act is, in essence, a victimless crime
3. Blame the "victim" for negligence, i.e., the actual accident may have been staged but the circumstances were present for a real accident to occur
4. Blame the "victim" for mistreating the suspect
5. Blame the media for giving the suspect the idea by publicizing similar claims
6. Blame another person (the doctor, lawyer, neighbor) for encouraging the subject to file the false claim
7. Blame the suspect's decision to file a false claim on his inability to earn a living
8. Blame unusual life circumstances, i.e., unable to earn a living due to a past criminal record, little education, drug or alcohol addiction, etc., for causing the subject's decision to file the false claim
9. Minimize the dollar amount of the claim
10. Contrast the suspect as a one-time offender versus someone who does this kind of thing all of the time

Theme example: Mary fakes falling on water that she intentionally put on a restaurant floor. Her intentions are to seek a $5,000 cash settlement.

"Mary, we know that you are faking the fall in the restaurant with the intent of a cash settlement. I think the reason that you did it is simply because you needed money due to your personal situation. We know that you've been out of work for the last six months and that can cause a great deal of anxiety and stress on a person. That stress and anxiety can cause someone that's honest to do something that's questionable. It's obvious this restaurant has a lot of money and I'm sure that your thinking was that it's not like taking money from someone that desperately needs it. Sometimes when people fake claims like this, it's generally not just one time but hundreds of times; their goal is to get rich, to make a living out of it. I'm sure you've talked to people that have done similar things that have made a lot of money. What they didn't tell you is that claims are investigated, just like we're doing now. As I said, Mary, we know the fall was intentionally staged. In investigations like this, employees are questioned, customers are questioned and video surveillance is reviewed. Nobody is disputing the fact that you fell, but we know the fall was deliberate. We also know that your witness, who you deny knowing, is actually your sister-in-law. Mary, when you intentionally fell, did you have a dollar amount in mind that you thought this restaurant would pay or were you hoping they would give you a little money and drop the matter?"

D. Worker's compensation fraud themes:

Most suspects involved in this crime do not view their behavior as criminal in nature. In fact, most suspects believe that anyone else in their situation would have done the same thing. Individuals who perpetrate this fraud and who are employed in certain labor-intensive industries believe that this behavior is the norm rather than the exception. Their belief is that the employer would rather replace the legitimately injured employee than to accept responsibility for the injuries. Additionally, if the suspect's job tends to be seasonal, another element in an effort to obtain some sense of financial security is introduced. Therefore, minimizing the suspect's behavior is not that difficult. The following theme selections serve to minimize behavior or shift the blame.

1. Minimize the duration of the event, comparing "just six months"

versus someone trying to perpetrate the scam for six years

2. Minimize the dollar amount involved, i.e., $1,500 versus $15,000

3. Blame peer pressure (someone else suggested the idea)

4. Blame the attending physician for agreeing to do the suspect a favor by falsifying the medical reports

5. Blame the fact that the suspect's age (e.g. 50 years old) made it very difficult for him to continue his normal workload, contrasting it with a 21-year-old who would be doing it just for the money

6. Blame the fact that the company had very poor controls in place to prevent such a claim; there was very little follow-up or checking by anyone

7. Blame the economy for not providing available work

8. Blame the fact that it is so easy to engage in this type of behavior

9. Suggest that anyone would engage in this behavior if the circumstances were right

10. Compliment the suspect for working on other occasions when he could have legitimately qualified for worker's compensation but failed to do so

11. Suggest that the government expects or understands that some corruption exists with these types of claims

12. Blame stress, alcohol or drugs for causing the person to make a bad decision

13. Contrast a situation in which the individual sustains an actual injury (albeit outside of the workplace) versus a person who has no injury whatsoever and is fabricating the entire claim

14. Contrast taking advantage of an individual (company) versus the government

15. Suggest that the injury may have been caused outside the workplace but was actually aggravated during work hours

16. Suggest that no one (else) was hurt or injured

17. Suggest that the subject's initial intent was just to challenge or test

the system, but then unusual circumstances (such as medical expenses, inclement weather causing working outside difficult, etc.) caused the act to continue

18. Suggest that the suspect wanted to get even with the employer for some prior mistreatment, i.e., the act of revenge

Intelligence Themes

"There is one evil I dread, and that is their spies. I wish, therefore, the most attentive watch be kept..."

George Washington

A. Unauthorized disclosure or storage of classified information:

1. Blame the "victim" for making their security procedures too restrictive – not allowing work to be taken home or saved to personal storage

2. Blame the influence of alcohol at a social function contributing to the subject's lack of judgment in divulging sensitive information

3. Blame the suspect's carelessness (such as talking too loudly on the phone or allowing others to view his computer screen or for not following proper security procedures while on the Internet) as opposed to someone who intentionally disclosed the information

4. Contrast with a more serious act, such as espionage

5. Contrast doing it a few times versus many times

6. Contrast receiving money for the information versus not receiving money for the disclosure

7. Suggest that the suspect's intent was simply to impress someone

8. Suggest that the disclosed material was not that sensitive; suggest that, in fact, the suspect may have thought that he heard the same information discussed by officials in the media

9. Suggest that the suspect simply wanted a souvenir

10. Suggest that a basic aspect of human nature is that we all make mistakes

11. Suggest that the material eventually could be obtained under "Freedom of Information"

12. Suggest that the suspect was forced to work on too many projects at one time and needed to store/bring home information so as not to fall behind on his work

13. Suggest that the suspect was in the process of moving and misplaced several items

14. Suggest that the subject's spouse or family members may have accidentally discarded information or discovered classified information by accident and subsequently shared it with others

15. Suggest that the suspect believed that the public had the right to know

16. Suggest that the suspect was tricked by the recipient to provide specific information

17. Suggest that the suspect thought that he was talking "off the record"

18. Suggest that the suspect did not provide information, but rather was simply validating what the recipient already knew

19. Suggest that the majority of the material the suspect provided was misinformation but that he decided to add a few pieces of real information for credibility

20. Suggest that the suspect owed a favor to the media in return for important information the media had supplied to the suspect in the past

B. Failure to report foreign national contacts:

1. Blame too much "red tape" or an unrealistic amount of time to process the report about something that the subject believed was unimportant

2. Blame alcohol for clouding the subject's judgment and contributing to the subsequent decision not to report the contact

3. Blame the subject's fear of consequence (loss of job, loss of security clearance, becoming the focus of an investigation) for causing him to make the decision not to report the contact

4. Blame the subject's fear of the consequences he might face for not reporting the contact in a timely manner

5. Blame the suspect's laziness

6. Suggest that the deterrent value of the polygraph test was lost due to the fact that it seemed too distant in the future

7. Contrast just a casual conversation versus a clandestine meeting

8. Exaggerate the number of contacts that the suspect failed to report

9. Exaggerate the number of times that the suspect failed to report

10. Suggest that the suspect intentionally failed to report a contact for fear of a mole (double agent) being inside the suspect's organization

11. Suggest that the suspect had doubts as to whether or not the contact was a foreign national

12. Suggest that the suspect was approached by the contact and that he did not initiate the meeting

13. Suggest that the suspect was simply curious to see how receptive the contact was to engage in a social dialogue but that no sensitive information was discussed or disclosed

14. Suggest that the suspect was conducting his own investigation and planned to report the contact if any relevant information was obtained

15. Suggest that the suspect simply forgot to report the contact

16. Suggest that nothing sensitive was discussed

17. Suggest that the contact was made during the suspect's personal time versus while on duty or during working hours

18. Suggest that the suspect's perception was that his colleagues might believe he was in collusion with the contact if it was

reported

19. Suggest that the suspect thought that there was no operational advantage to report the meeting(s)

20. Suggest that the suspect told the foreign national that he would not report the contact in an effort to establish greater trust and credibility in the hopes of obtaining sensitive information from the contact at future meetings (further imply that the suspect was concerned that if he did report the contact, the foreign national might learn of it, thereby undermining the suspect's credibility)

C. Espionage:

1. Blame the fact that the institution (organization) had very poor security or lacked proper controls for the protection of information

2. Blame the need for money – unexpected bills, education, frozen wages, anticipated promotion that was not received, excessive medical bills, spouse's lost job, incurring relocation expenses that were much more costlier than anticipated, overextended vacation expenses, too much credit card debt, gambling, lifestyle, alimony, realization pension would not provide adequate retirement, inheritance below what was expected, etc.

3. Blame the influence of alcohol for causing the suspect to make poor decisions

4. Blame the influence of stress – perhaps the subject could not live up to his family's expectations, anxiety about spending too much time away from home, the pressure imposed by the nature of the job, etc.

5. Blame the organization for mistreating the suspect (no promotion, no special recognition, etc.) suggesting that this was essentially an act of revenge versus something that was done with the intent of harming individuals or the country

6. Blame the frustration and anxiety caused by the employer's "unethical" or "amoral" activities towards certain individuals or countries

7. Suggest that the amount of money or valuables promised was just too tempting

8. Suggest that the suspect was conducting his own investigation

9. Suggest that the suspect believed that the information he gave out was within proper parameters and was not ultra-sensitive in nature

10. Suggest that the suspect was blackmailed – that he was threatened to provide the information or suffer severe consequences

11. Suggest that the suspect's initial intent was to remove classified information to simply work on or complete a project at home

12. Suggest that the suspect thought that the policy was unclear

13. Suggest that the suspect's initial intention in securing the information was to write a book when material became less sensitive, but that in the meantime an unusual event (unexpected expenses, job frustration, etc.) caused the suspect to act out of character and use the information in this manner

14. Suggest that the "victim" (US intelligence employee) was initially overheard discussing classified information with a colleague and was subsequently blackmailed by the "enemy"

15. Suggest that the suspect initially provided rather innocuous information to the contact and, in return, received a gift, after which his acceptance of the gift was then used to pressure him to provide additional information or to be exposed to his employer

16. Suggest that the suspect was seduced into the situation and subsequently blackmailed to provide information

17. Suggest that the suspect believed that the information he disclosed would not be detrimental to our country or individuals

18. Suggest that the suspect was under medication and that, combined with the alcohol he consumed, caused him to say things he

definitely would not have said had he been sober

19. Suggest that the suspect was bragging in an effort to show his importance

20. Suggest that the suspect was simply asked to validate information that was already known

21. Suggest that the suspect believed that he was giving the information to a "friendly" country

22. Suggest that the suspect's actions and the information sold were actually helpful to our government by allowing us to identifying U.S. agents spying for the foreign country (recipient of information)

23. Contrast a situation in which the subject was providing information for just a short time (e.g., one year) versus repeatedly over several years

24. Contrast whether or not the subject went out and solicited the contact versus the contact approaching the subject

Example: A 20-year federal employee sells classified information to a foreign national on ten separate occasions over the last two years.

"There is no doubt that you have sold classified information but our concern has to do with the frequency that you have done this and the true reason as to why you did this. You have been with our agency for twenty years with high-level clearance for the entire time. We know for sure that you have sold information at various times over the last two years but our concern is whether or not you have been doing this over your entire career – over the last twenty years. If it has been for the entire twenty years then that would indicate that you very probably got the job here for the purpose of doing tremendous harm to our country and our military without any regard whatsoever for anyone but yourself. And another concern we have is exactly who initiated the contact about selling certain documents. Our experience shows us that there are generally two kinds of people that sell this type of information. One type is the person that intentionally uses his position to profit with total disregard to his colleagues and country. The other type is a person who is an honest, hard-working person who, because of an unusual set of circumstances, does something totally out of character. We are trying to determine which one of these individuals you are.

"I think you were befriended by an individual that knew your clearance level and the access that you had to certain information. In other words, there is a chance that you were profiled and that this thing got started with you supplying very low-grade information or information that was not classified. As you and your friend became more comfortable, things probably escalated. Low-grade information requests increased to classified requests. I also think that you believed that the information you began to provide would not cause the death of any of your colleagues. However, the more this thing continued, the more you realized that you couldn't stop. Even though you wanted to stop, they wouldn't let you. Your friend literally owned you. Your friend probably asked you to do 'one more favor,' but there never was just one more favor. In addition, we know that you had two other factors occurring in your life causing you to act out of character. First, we know you were overextended with your mortgage and equity line of credit, as well as credit card debt due to some unusual family expenses. Second, the promotions and accompanying raises that you expected didn't materialize. The combined ingredients of need and opportunity caused you to act out of character.

"Our concern is this. Are we right in thinking that you were solicited or profiled to sell classified information? Was it only for a brief two-year period and not over the whole twenty years? Was it the result of some unusual family expenses and not greed? Was it also because of the fact that you didn't get a fair shake from the organization – you never got the promotions or compensation you expected? The final and most important question is this – do you have a total disregard for your colleagues and country? Do you? Or are you an honest guy that made one poor judgment and things got out of hand?"

D. Wrongful destruction/bomb threats:

1. Blame the organization for mistreating the subject (demotion, being overly critical of the suspect, etc.)
2. Blame peer pressure
3. Blame alcohol or drugs for impaired judgment
4. Contrast the subject's behavior with a more serious offense such as an act of sabotage in which people were severely injured
5. Praise the suspect for not doing something more serious
6. Praise the suspect's courage and moral convictions for consummating the act – doing something that most people thought about but were afraid to do
7. Praise the suspect for having an exemplary work record
8. Suggest that the suspect's intent was to test the security system
9. Minimize the suspect's behavior by suggesting that the act was not executed
10. Minimize the loss (to property or individuals)
11. Suggest that the suspect's intent was to draw attention to poor maintenance or security problems
12. Suggest that the suspect's intent was to get time off by shutting down a facility
13. Suggest that the act was nothing more than a joke
14. Suggest that the suspect did not understand the actual consequences of the act
15. Suggest the act was an accident (this should be a last resort theme as it may become a defense; however, the suspect's credibility may be challenged for denying any involvement or having previously lied under oath)

E. Order and discipline investigations:

For example, failure to report attending a meeting of an organization intending to disrupt US activities or to commit illegal activities, such as the KKK, militia, Al Qaeda, Neo-Nazi, etc.

1. Right to attend – 1st amendment
2. Doing your own investigation
3. Peer pressure to attend meetings
4. Joke
5. One time versus several, just to see what it is all about

Juvenile Themes

Certain states have statutes that specifically prescribe the condition under which juvenile suspects may be interrogated. If the juvenile's parent or guardian will be present during the interview or interrogation, the investigator should first meet with the parent to establish the interview/interrogation guidelines. Prior to the non-accusatory interview the parent should be advised that the purpose of the interview is to question his son/daughter regarding the specific incident. The parent is further advised that his son's/daughter's answers to the questions are important and to refrain from interrupting. The parent is welcomed during the interview to act as an observer. The parent is further informed that if his son/daughter was not involved in the incident, the investigator wants to establish that and therefore, the parent is asked to refrain from interrupting. Following the interview, both the investigator and the juvenile's parent should step out of the interview room.

If the juvenile is believed to be deceptive, the parent should be advised. The parent is informed that it is the investigator's opinion that his son/daughter has not told the whole truth regarding the issue under investigation. The investigator welcomes the parent to return to the interview room. It is important that the investigator sit approximately four or five feet directly in front of the juvenile. The parent should be seated next to and slightly behind his son/daughter.   This seating arrangement prevents the juvenile from being forced to look directly at his parent's disappointment, disbelief or disgust of the situation. The juvenile is insulated from these emotions by only having to view the investigator.

The interrogation should begin by the investigator advising the parent in the presence of the juvenile that his son/daughter has not told the whole truth. The parent will generally want to believe that his son/daughter did not commit the crime and approaching the realization that his son/daughter committed the crime may have a devastating effect. The misbehavior of his child may cause the parent to think that they failed in raising their child. The parent, as well as the son/daughter, needs focus on the interrogator's themes with the intent of allowing the parent to save dignity and respect. In this situation, the investigator should begin by addressing themes directly to the parent and not the juvenile. The initial themes should excuse the parent from viewing himself as a failure. One such theme would be to blame peer pressure for his son's/daughter's behavior.   Once the parent appears to be listening to the theme, the interrogator should direct the themes toward the juvenile. The following is a brief example:

(Interrogator facing and talking to the parent) "Mr. Smith, it is our opinion that Corey did not tell us the whole truth regarding the fire in the high school's washroom. Fortunately, and most importantly, no one was killed or even injured. Yes, there was some superficial damage to the washroom, but there was no major structural damage.   All things considered, we are all very fortunate things turned out the way they did. I'm sure that you raised Corey to obey the law and to always do the right thing. In fact, that is the same way I raised my children. That is the way my parents raised me and I'm sure, your parents raised you. It sometimes

doesn't matter how hard a parent tries in setting proper examples for their children. Sometimes our kids hang out with friends that haven't had the same caring and concerned parents like us. Sometimes our kids hang out with some really bad friends, friends that can influence good kids into doing something that they normally would never do. In other words, Mr. Smith, some kids are brought up not having the same respect for others that we try to instill in our children. When that happens, our kids can find themselves doing something that they normally would never do. That is what I think happened here."

The parent begins to nod in agreement. The interrogator turns his attention to the juvenile since the parent is beginning to accept the theme, which removes the blame from the parents and begins to place it on the suspect's friends.

"Corey, do you understand what I'm trying to say? I think your mom and dad really care about you; otherwise they wouldn't be here. I don't think you set the fire without being influenced by others, just to see their reaction. I also don't think that you wanted to burn the entire school down or kill every person in the building. I think it was a situational thing where at the moment you thought it was funny. I'm not interested right now who put you up to this, but it's really important for us to know whether or not this was done just as a joke or were you really trying to burn down the school and hurt the students and teachers? From talking to you and your caring parents, I really don't think that was the case. I think that you were just looking for a reaction from your peers, weren't you? You didn't want to kill anyone, did you? This was just a juvenile prank, wasn't it?"

Juvenile interrogation themes:

1. Suggest that the interrogator's intent is to identify and correct a minor problem before it escalates into something more serious,

e.g., an auto theft in which no one was hurt versus an auto theft which results in a death during a hit-and-run

2. Suggest that the younger the individual is, the more likely it is that he will make mistakes or exhibit poor judgment, e.g., auto insurance is higher for teenagers because they are expected to make mistakes or display poor judgment

3. Blame the multitude of temptations that exist today versus during the youth's parents' era

4. Blame the media, movies, or video games for desensitizing youth to criminal behavior

5. Blame the victim's actions and behavior, i.e., being abusive, careless, aggressive, arrogant or dishonest for provoking the suspect's response

6. Blame alcohol or drugs as compounding the suspect's poor judgment

7. Blame the suspect's extreme hormonal changes for causing him to act out of character

8. Describe the suspect's intentions as simply trying to experience the thrill or excitement of the activity, or simply wanting to see the reaction of others, as opposed to the intention of trying to seriously hurt someone

9. Blame the community in which the juvenile lives for not providing adequate organized programs, i.e., sporting events, hobby clubs, Big Brothers, etc.

10. If the parent is not present during the interrogation, after developing the theme, the investigator may ask the suspect, "Do you want to explain to your parents what you did (meaning the crime), or do you want me to explain what you did to your parents?" The suspect has made his first initial admission if he chooses either option. If the suspect asks the investigator to explain the crime to his parents, the investigator needs to obtain corroborating details from the suspect. If the suspect chooses to

tell his parents he committed the crime, the investigator should again begin to establish details of the crime from the suspect.

11. Minimize the juvenile's behavior
    a. Peer pressure, suggesting that the juvenile went along with others versus this being his idea
    b. Suggest gang initiation caused the offender to act out of character, suggesting that the suspect was forced to commit the crime out of fear of retaliation for not committing the crime
    c. Suggest that the act was necessary to provide for his family or friends
    d. Suggest that no one was hurt
    e. Compliment the suspect for not using a weapon
    f. Compliment the suspect for not taking a life
    g. Compliment the suspect for not causing permanent injury
    h. Compliment the suspect for not planning the act
    i. Contrast doing something like this one time versus many times
    j. Contrast the suspect as being a misunderstood youth versus a hardened criminal

12. Blame the juvenile's parents for
    a. Their lack of supervision, working too much, never at home, never paying attention to the suspect's needs
    b. Creating a very stressful home environment through their divorce or separation
    c. Not providing any love or affection
    d. Not being a proper role model – using drugs, shoplifting, drinking, etc.
    e. Not providing the basic necessities of life such as food, clothing, proper medical care, etc.
    f. Not providing a meaningful allowance for the suspect
    g. Not accepting the suspect's friends

    h.   Showing favoritism to other siblings

    i.   Being physically or verbally abusive to the suspect

    j.   Forcing the suspect to leave home by creating an unbearable environment

Kidnapping Themes

Ransom is perhaps the primary motive for kidnapping. Ransom is also one of the least reprehensible motives for kidnapping. Therefore, contrast the intent of ransom with the more egregious motives such as sex trafficking, selling for body parts or selling to wanting parents. Furthermore, if the victim is not killed, themes should be contrasted with the more serious offense of homicide. If however, the victim has been killed, homicide or even terrorist themes discussed in this book may be referenced for additional options.

A. Contrast the motive of ransom with:

1. Sexually assaulting the victim
2. Killing or inflicting bodily harm
3. An elaborate scheme to satisfy a political agenda
4. Terrorist intent
5. Forcing the victim to perform unlawful acts

B. Blame the victim or victim's family, employer or country for:

1. Poor security measures, making it easy for the kidnapping to occur
2. Inadequate supervision of the victim
3. Exhibiting oppressive behaviors
4. Detrimental political views

5. Engaging in unethical or illegal business practices
6. Flaunting their excessive wealth
7. Unfair competition
8. Not responding to or taking prior threats seriously

C. Minimize the offense by suggesting that:

1. The amount of the ransom requested was reasonable
2. The suspect was willing to negotiate a release
3. The suspect did not detain the victim for a very long time
4. The suspect provided appropriate treatment for the victim
5. This was not a common practice of the offender but rather a single, isolated situation
6. The suspect's peers pressured him into doing this
7. The suspect was threatened to perform the act of kidnapping
8. The intentions of the offender were honorable
9. The offender's intent was to release the hostage unharmed even if the ransom was never paid
10. Alcohol, drugs or stress caused the suspect to act out of character
11. The offender's emotions (anger, fear, revenge, envy, etc.) caused the suspect to misjudge the seriousness of the act
12. The media is at fault for glamorizing or publicizing the offense

Theme example: Mick and Patty, both in their twenties, abduct a six-month-old infant named Kelly from a shopping mall. After three days they panic and abandon the baby in a cardboard box on the steps of a Catholic church. A bystander saw a young woman putting a box on the church steps and was able to record a partial license plate of the vehicle. Mick and Patty are one of three people in the area with the plate numbers reported. Mick and Patty claim they can't remember if they were at the mall on the date of the abduction.

"Patty, we know that your car was observed leaving the church where the baby Kelly was found. We also have the video from the security camera showing you at the mall the day the baby was taken. The question, Patty, is no longer if you and Mick took the baby, but rather why. In cases like this, babies are taken for a variety of reasons – to teach the parents a lesson for their lack of supervision, for ransom money, to sell, to raise as their own, or worse yet, to sell for body parts.

"I know from talking to both you and Mick that you've been married for a few years and have no children. I also know that you and Mick are good people and have a nice house. Unfortunately, I'm also aware that recently you had a miscarriage. The desire for some people to have children is extremely strong and can sometimes become an obsession. I'm beginning to think that this was something that was caused by pure emotion and poor judgment as a direct result of your miscarriage. Our experience in situations like this is that something very stressful occurs in a person's life, as in your situation, causing good people to overreact out of emotion. I'm also beginning to think that this was the first time that you and Mick ever did anything like this, and I certainly don't think you were in the business of selling infants for ritualistic acts, or body parts. I'm sure you've read about things like that happening.

"By the looks of Kelly, you and Mick took really good care of her. That tells me that you probably planned on keeping her for yourself and not harming or selling her. And looking at the fact that you left her on the church steps tells me that you wanted someone trustworthy to find her immediately so no harm would come to her. Sometimes we all do things that are uncharacteristic and irrational. That is what I believe happened with you and Mick. I don't think you stalked Kelly; in fact, you probably wouldn't have taken her had the parents provided more supervision, love or affection towards her.

"Our concern, Patty, is was this done to hold her for ransom or did you just take her because you thought that you could give her a better life? I don't think that you and Mick were going to hold her for ransom, or do something very bad to her, were you?"

Knowledge Themes

Obtaining knowledge from an individual that did not directly commit the crime can in some cases be more difficult than obtaining an admission from the primary offender. There are several reasons why an individual who possesses knowledge of the perpetrator's identity is reluctant to implicate that person. The primary motivation to conceal his knowledge is typically fear of retribution from the perpetrator to either him or his family members. Other reasons for concealing the offender's identity may include concern about eventually having to testify; implicating a friend, relative or coworker; or simply being labeled a "snitch." The primary theme development in obtaining an admission of guilty knowledge should be to focus on minimizing the act (of concealing knowledge) by contrasting or minimizing "only having knowledge" versus being the primary offender.

A. Primary themes:

1. Minimize the seriousness of the primary offender's actions or behavior
2. Minimize the frequency of the activities committed by the primary offender
3. Minimize the suspect's involvement as only having knowledge versus being the primary offender
4. Suggest that the suspect just learned about the offender's behavior after the act as opposed to being present when the crime was committed

5. Suggest the suspect was present when the crime was perpetrated but had no prior knowledge the offense was to occur

6. Suggest to the subject that if the situation were reversed, the primary offender would definitely implicate him

7. Blame the primary offender for bragging that he committed the crime

8. Blame others for telling the subject the primary offender's name

9. Compliment the suspect for not participating in the crime

10. Compliment the suspect for being loyal to the primary offender

B. Secondary themes:

1. Suggest to the suspect that the name or names of the primary offender(s) are already known and the interrogator only needs to hear them from the suspect to validate the full extent of his cooperation

2. Suggest that because of the natural inclination "not to get involved" the interrogator can understand the suspect's initial reluctance to implicate the primary offender

3. Suggest that as the investigation continues the primary offender may falsely implicate the suspect

4. Suggest to the suspect that eventually someone will talk and that you will believe who talks first

5. Suggest to the suspect that the real reason he is reluctant to identify the primary offender is because he would be implicating himself as the person who committed the crime

C. Last resort themes:

1. Tell the suspect that you do not need to know the complete name of the primary offender but just his initials, thereby allowing the suspect to maintain the position that he never said the perpetrator's name

2. Show the suspect a list of potential primary offender names and ask him to signal the right name by pointing a pen at the correct name or by coughing, clearing his throat, whistling or looking away when the correct name is mentioned, thereby allowing the suspect to maintain the position that he never said the perpetrator's name

3. Advise the suspect to write down the name(s) of those involved while the investigator leaves the interview room, thereby allowing the suspect to maintain the position that he did not say the name to the investigator

4. Present a hypothetical argument to the suspect, that if he had children having such knowledge, what would his advice be to his children be – to lie or to tell the truth

Once the suspect makes the initial admission of implicating the offender, the interrogator should obtain the details that will serve to substantiate the suspect's knowledge. The suspect will be reluctant to share this information, but once the ice is broken with the first admission, additional details will be usually be revealed. The interrogator might suggest to the suspect that he has already taken the first and most difficult step in showing his cooperation. Subsequent themes should focus on minimizing the suspect's involvement in the crime.

Theme example: Mae is arrested for selling cocaine. She states that she bought the cocaine that she was reselling from an unknown dealer on the street.

"Mae, there is no doubt that you know the name of the person that you bought your coke from. I can understand why you're reluctant to give this person's name. First of all, there is a street code of ethics of not being the rat. I can appreciate your allegiance to this person. But if things were reversed and you were the main dealer, your sellers would give up your name in a heartbeat. The question is not whether or not you're being disloyal, Mae; the question is how much does Mae want to cooperate? If you're small time, selling just enough to make ends meet, not making tens of thousands of dollars, that needs to be explained. You see, Mae, I don't want somebody to try to say you're one of the main dealers! I don't think you are but I can't say that for sure.

"We know the names of several of the main dealers, but we're not going to share those names with you. By the same token, we're not going to give them your name. But by confirming for us who these guys are, will show the full extent of your cooperation. If, on the other hand, you give us the name of someone that we know is not selling drugs, an innocent person, then we'll know that you're not cooperating.

"You know, Mae, you very well might be giving us the name of someone who will eventually want to cooperate with us and give us his supplier. These people don't care about you or anyone! They only care about your money. They don't live by a code of ethics; they live by a code of money. There is only one person you should care about and that's you. You see, other people have cooperated with us and I'm not telling you what others have said; that information is confidential. Mae, how many people are you buying your coke from, more or less than a dozen?"

Money Laundering Themes

Money laundering is the process of taking illegally obtained money and giving it the appearance that it was generated from a legitimate source. This offense is usually the end result of prior criminal activity. Instances in which this activity may occur would include tax evasion, drug dealing, arms dealing and organized corruption. This money is put through one or more transactions to have it ultimately appear as though it was obtained legally. The intent of this crime is to provide the offender with what appears to be a legitimate cover for this income. Offenders generally consider this fraudulent creation of wealth as a victimless crime. Consequently, the interrogator may capitalize on this perception by developing themes that primarily contrast the suspect's involvement in the more serious primary crime of dealing drugs, tax evasion, etc., versus just being involved in making money appear legitimate.

Primary motives of money laundering include:

    A. Providing what appears to be a legitimate cover for illegal income
    B. Artificially increasing profits
    C. An effort to avoid the seizure of assets
    D. An effort to avoid prosecution
    E. Tax evasion

Theme selection should attempt to address the primary motive of the offense. The interrogator must determine which of the following suggestions would be the most appropriate given the specifics of the case.

1. Since money laundering generally involves the participation of several individuals to accomplish this crime, the interrogator should consider playing one against the other. The development of the theme should focus on emphasizing to the suspect that in cases like this, someone always talks – someone will eventually tell the truth (or at least their version of it) and that this is his opportunity to show his cooperation by telling the truth, even if he indicates only a minor involvement in the scheme. Imply to the suspect that when that occurs (when the first person "talks"), it may be too late for people to believe that the suspect, as he may then claim, was just following instructions or that he was involved for only a short time or even that it wasn't his idea. It

may be further suggested to the suspect that the only reason he would not want to tell the truth now is because he masterminded the scheme.

2. Suggest that the suspect was only involved in the administration of the financial transactions from the unlawful activity and was not directly involved in the illegal act.

3. Suggest that the suspect discovered the proceeds used in the financial transactions were illegally obtained only after or during the legitimate financial transactions

4. Suggest that the suspect was in fear of retribution if he did not implement the laundering process

5. Suggest to the suspect that he knew that the laundered money was the result of a crime in which no one was physically hurt

6. Suggest that the laundered money was necessary to prevent a company's bankruptcy, thereby protecting people from otherwise losing their jobs

7. In cases that involve the conversion of charitable donations to personal income, the interrogator should minimize the dollar amount that was involved in the conversion as compared to the dollar amount that was maintained in the charitable account

8. In cases that involve obtaining loans through the use of false financial statements (bank fraud) or in cases which involve the authorization of the transfer of fraudulent loan proceeds to pay off a balance on a legitimate outstanding loan, blame the greed of the financial institution or the carelessness of their security procedures

9. Blame the organization or company officials for "forcing" the suspect to engage in this activity by the pressure that they exerted on him to make a profit

10. Blame investor greed for creating an environment in which it was easy to obtain money illegally

11. Compliment the suspect for using the illegally obtained money

for good reasons, i.e., to pay off a home mortgage or a car loan as opposed to "bad" reasons such as living a lavish lifestyle, drugs, gambling, etc.

12. Blame the suspect for getting involved in this activity as a result of a lifestyle that was out of control

13. Blame the fact that the laws defining money laundering were unclear

14. Blame the ease with which the process can be accomplished

15. Blame unjust and unfair government taxation policies for creating the "need" to engage in such activity

16. Blame the influence of friends or business associates for getting the suspect to engage in this activity

17. Minimize the amount of money involved and/or the time period over which the laundering activity occurred

18. Compliment the suspect for paying taxes on the illegally obtained money

19. Compliment the suspect for no longer engaging in the activity that produced the illegally obtained money or in the money laundering activity itself

20. Compliment the suspect for being a basically good person, i.e., a hard worker, no or few criminal convictions, taxpayer, exemplary parent, respected community leader, etc.

Occult Themes

These crimes may involve ritualistic behavior against animals or human beings. If human death occurs, homicide could be referenced for optional themes.

Primary themes:

1. Blame peer pressure for encouraging the suspect to join and engage in the cult activity

2. Suggest that the excitement or intensity of the moment caused the suspect to act without thinking

3. Minimize the seriousness of the act – contrast the fact that the "victim" was an animal as opposed to a human being

4. Blame the suspect's intense interest in spirituality for influencing his decision

5. Psychologically justify the suspect's victimization of animals by pointing out that the Bible suggests that animals were put on earth to serve man

6. Blame alcohol or drugs for clouding the suspect's judgment

7. Blame the Internet for glamorizing this type of behavior

8. Contrast the behavior as being something that the suspect has only engaged in for a short period of time (months) versus over a much longer time period such as years

9. Suggest that the offender was raised in a difficult family situation (physically or verbally abusive, alcoholic parent(s), extreme religious beliefs, etc.), which ultimately served as the catalyst for the offender's behavior – it seemed normal

10. Suggest that the offender was "forced" to commit the crime by either physical threats or demeaning verbal statements which challenged the suspect's manhood

Theme example: Fred is suspected of torturing animals and leaving occult material in a park near his home.

"Fred, I think that the reason you got involved in the occult was really because your friends talked you into it. Sometimes friends can pressure us into doing something that we would normally never do on our own. Not too many people know anything about this kind of stuff so the natural curiosity we all have makes it difficult to refuse when we have the opportunity to find out about it. It's different, intriguing and interesting whether or not you believe in it. In fact, certain religions have some very unique practices and   ceremonies and what a person believes in is ultimately an individual choice.

"Unfortunately, a lot of people associate the occult with what they see on TV or in the movies where it is usually portrayed as something truly evil and bizarre. When people see or read about what went on in the park the other night they immediately begin to wonder if babies are going to be next. People become paranoid, especially with the way the newspaper and TV reports portrayed the situation. People understandably tend to overreact to what they don't really know about. Our concern is whether or not you're just experimenting with this kind of thing (the occult) or if this really has developed into something on the next level that involves hurting a child or an adult, or even doing something much worse. I'd like to think that this is the extent of your experimentation. It is, isn't it Fred?"

Passport Fraud Themes

1. Blame the government policy for placing unfair restrictions on certain countries
2. Blame someone else for minimizing the seriousness of the act or suggesting that this is a common practice
3. Minimize the uniqueness of this activity by comparing passport fraud with truck drivers possessing multiple driver's licenses or teenagers possessing illegal IDs
4. Minimize the offender's motive for using an illegal passport, i.e., his intent was to expedite entry versus committing a terrorist act
5. Psychologically minimize the suspect's culpability by contrasting stealing the passport versus just finding it or being given the fraudulent passport

6. Minimize the offender's behavior by contrasting just using a fraudulent passport versus counterfeiting passports

7. Suggest that the suspect was just trying see if he could overcome the challenge of entering the country with a falsified identity

8. Suggest that the offender did not have the proper identification to obtain a legal passport in a timely manner so he perpetrated the fraud only as a means to expedite the process versus doing it to facilitate the commission of a criminal act

9. Suggest that because the offender has done this before as a matter of routine he no longer thought of the act as illegal or unusual

10. Suggest that the offender acted out of desperation, i.e., the suspect was from a country that restricted entry to the U.S. and was forced to use an illegal passport for good reasons, such as, to pay respects to a loved one that died in the restricted country

Theme example: Roberto is stopped entering the country with a fraudulent Canadian passport. He claims that he lost his original passport, went to a government office in Canada, filled out the paperwork and was issued this replacement. There is no record from Canadian authorities that Roberto reported a lost passport or completed any paperwork to have his passport reissued. The passport is a forgery.

"Roberto, there is no doubt that you knew this passport was an 'imitation' (the word counterfeit is avoided during the interrogation, as it connotes a serious crime and thus serious consequences) and not real. I think the reason that you used this imitation was because you knew that since 9/11 our country's policy of allowing entry to foreigners is becoming much more difficult. This very restrictive policy is not designed to cause good people grief, but to protect against terrorists entering the country. Unfortunately, in protecting our borders, it sometimes makes it nearly impossible for people like yourself who are entering not to harm anyone, but perhaps to be reunited with family or friends or even to try to make a living in our country.

"I know that your description doesn't match any known terrorist that we're trying to catch. We also know that there are many such people that we don't have any information on. I really don't think that you were entering the country to cause harm, but as I said previously, perhaps your intent is to be with family or friends. Generally when someone uses an imitation passport, it's usually because someone else sold him the imitation passport. I'm sure they also told you how easy it would be to use. However, the people that sell you the passport either don't know or care to tell you about all of the extra precautions we've implemented since 9/11. All they care about is taking your money and they're gone.

"Our concern, Roberto, is whether or not you hurt someone to get their passport and altered it or did you simply buy it from someone? Another and perhaps more important concern is whether or not you were entering the country to meet up with friends or family or if you were entering to commit an act of terrorism. First, did you steal the passport or just buy it from someone?"

Piracy Themes

These themes address the theft of audio products, video products, software, etc.

A. Themes for reproducing or selling:

1. Blame the manufacturer for their poor product security, suggesting that there was little or no embedded security in the product, thereby making duplication easy

2. Blame the monopolistic behavior of the manufacturer/artist

3. Blame someone else for approaching the suspect to copy software/music

4. Blame software manufacturers for providing the means to circumvent the law

5. Blame the ease with which the act can be accomplished, for example, via the Internet

6. Blame the lack of enforcement regarding this type of violation; suggest that the suspect thought there was an unwritten understanding that piracy would be tolerated as long as it was not conducted on a large scale

7. Blame the lack of clarity or the many varied interpretations of international copyright laws

8. Blame poor judgment, the suspect's recent loss of his job, the unreasonably high cost of the original items, the suspect's need for income, unexpected family expenses, etc., for causing the suspect to act out of character

9. Blame the suspect's employer for not providing the necessary work-related software to do the job

10. Blame the suspect's employer for condoning the practice, either directly or indirectly

11. Suggest that the suspect's superior technical intellect was the genesis for causing him to see if he could overcome the challenges associated with duplicating the product

12. Minimize the profit that the suspect made

13. Minimize the frequency in which the suspect engaged in this type of activity

14. Minimize the seriousness of the act by suggesting that the "victim" could afford the potential loss

15. Minimize the seriousness of the act by suggesting that the suspect did not hurt or steal from an individual

16. Suggest that everyone else is doing the same thing

17. Suggest to the suspect that he did it because of a dare
18. Suggest that the suspect's initial intent was for personal use or to have it as back-up software as opposed to selling it
19. Suggest that the suspect was helping others that could not afford the highly prohibitive prices of the original product
20. Suggest the buyer was trying to save sales tax
21. Suggest the buyer purchased the suspect's pirated products out of convenience
22. Suggest that if the suspect did not provide illegally copied products, others would
23. Suggest the suspect justified copying via "free use" copyright exceptions which applies to some educational software
24. Contrast the pirate-hobbyist versus the professional
25. Contrast shoplifting versus pirating
26. Contrast revenge against the original manufacturer versus making a few dollars
27. Contrast interstate versus intrastate delivery
28. Contrast United States versus worldwide distribution

B. Employee theft of proprietary information/pirating:

1. Blame the suspect's difficult financial circumstances (low wages, unusual family expenses, the high cost of living) for causing him to make a mistake in judgment
2. Blame poor security for giving the suspect the opportunity to do something he would not have looked to do otherwise
3. Blame the fact that the suspect has been mistreated by the employer
4. Refer to the section on employee theft themes for additional ideas

Theme example: John is a college student who has been making copies of DVD movies and CD software and selling them at flea markets.

"John, first of all let me make sure that you understand that we know that you have been selling CDs and DVDs that you made on your own. Our concern though is why you're doing it. We know that you're a good student but you haven't been able to get a scholarship to help defer the tremendous cost of tuition, room and board, as well as books. You and I both know what a store charges for a DVD or a CD! The prices are way out of line. Everyone who buys DVDs or CDs knows that he's being cheated on the price. The store, actors, producers and musicians are all making big bucks from the exorbitant sales prices.

"What you're doing is simply supplying a secondary market, a market of people that wouldn't purchase the original product. Also, John, we know that you're not getting rich off this, you're just making some side money to make ends meet at college.

"John, I don't think you got involved in breaking the codes on the software that prevent people from making copies. You probably just got a program off of the Internet that allows people to copy movies, music or software. Let's face it; if the manufacturers really wanted to stop people from copying their products, they would have developed security measures to prevent copying. Did they do this? No!

"If all you did was to provide a secondary market, mainly for friends, through word of mouth and not advertising on the Internet, then that needs to be explained. If you were using the Internet to sell the bootlegged copies then I'd have to say that this was not just to cover your college expenses, I'd say that this was your primary business. John, was this done on a small-time level to supplement your income or is this a million dollar operation?"

Polygraph Themes

These themes are designed for use during post-polygraph interrogations when deception is indicated – primarily following a pre-employment, periodic or clearance polygraph examination.

Up to this point, all of the themes described in this book are appropriate for criminal acts that may be the subject of a specific issue polygraph examination interrogation. When deception is indicated on a specific issue polygraph examination, the interrogation should not focus on the "test results" because the subject may simply debate the accuracy of the polygraph technique. Debating the instrument's reliability generally will not result in a confession; at most the interrogator may develop a minor admission. The investigator should, therefore, develop interrogation themes without referring to the polygraph test results.

With regard to a pre-employment or periodic/clearance polygraph examination interrogation, the subject should be advised that there was a *reaction* on a particular question, but that the *reaction* alone does not tell the whole truth.

When deception is indicated during a pre-employment polygraph question, for example, when the subject denies using illegal drugs during the last year, it should be explained that the polygraph test cannot determine what type of drug was used, or for that matter, the frequency of use, or why the suspect used the drug. The interrogation may proceed along the following lines:

"Brian, you showed a reaction to the drug question on the test and I would like to talk to you about that response. Generally, people think that they have to be perfect and many times think that just because they may have tried drugs at some time within the last year that it would automatically be grounds for not being considered for employment. My experience has been that people generally are too hard on themselves. What I mean is that most people believe that they have to be 100% perfect or else they won't get the job. The reality is that we all make mistakes and no one is perfect. I'd like you to consider that very seriously. I'm sure you would agree with me when I say that there is a difference between someone using heroin on a daily basis as opposed to using it a few times socially during the last year. There is also a difference between someone using heroin or other drugs during working hours as opposed to during break time or the lunch hour. Likewise, there is a difference in whether or not someone is using heroin, cocaine or marijuana. And furthermore, there is a difference between someone who uses drugs socially, due to dependency, or because of peer pressure, as opposed to someone who does it simply to enhance their job performance.

"You see, Brian, the polygraph cannot answer any of these questions, which is why I am talking to you today. Remember what I said earlier, no one is perfect. The most important thing is that we find out exactly what drugs you have tried in the last year so that if necessary, you can be retested and pass the polygraph examination. This will show that you are being completely truthful, which is most important. With that in mind, what drugs have you tried in the last year?"

Avoid the word "used" during the interrogation – suspects perceive "used" as having a negative connotation, such as repeated use of drugs. The word "tried" appears more socially acceptable in that it conveys occasional or experimental usage.

"With that in mind, Brian, what drugs have you just tried during the last year? Would it be heroin?"

Begin with a very socially unacceptable drug such as heroin. If the suspect answers "no," as opposed to giving a categorical denial such as "I haven't tried any drugs," the suspect in essence has validated his deception to the drug question. The interrogator should then proceed to suggest more socially acceptable drugs.

"Well then, Brian, are we just talking about cocaine?"

If the suspect hesitates or gives a weak or qualified denial, which may be exhibited by a delay in response or lack of eye contact, the interrogator should entertain the possibility that this was the drug being used by the suspect. If on the other hand, the suspect responds with yet another more immediate, direct denial, the interrogator should then suggest another drug. The question should be asked in an assumptive manner.

"Brian, are we just talking about amphetamine or speed?"

If the suspect hesitates or does not offer a denial, the interrogator should immediately follow up by asking an alternative question.

"Is that all we are talking about is just amphetamines and not heroin? Are we talking every day or just occasionally?   If it is occasionally, it is important to get that clarified."

If the suspect responds that he has used amphetamines, the interrogator should immediately respond with a follow-up question to seek an admission.

"Brian, have you tried any amphetamines today?"

There is an implied admission if the suspect responds, "no, not today."'

"Good, I didn't think so. When was the last time that you tried amphetamines? Was it this week?"

If the suspect denies usage this week, then introduce other time frames to determine the last time amphetamines were used.

"Was it last month?"

If the suspect nods his head or says yes, the investigator has obtained the first admission. The frequency should then be established by using the approximate number of days in the year.

"How many times in the last year would you estimate that you have tried amphetamines? If there are 365 days in a year and you have tried them every day, that would be 365 times. If you tried them twice a day, that would be about 700 times this year. If you tried them three times a day, that would be about 1,000 times in the last year. Using that as a guide, and being fair to yourself, what would be the most number of times that you believe that you have tried amphetamines in the last year? Is it possible it could be 1,000 times?"

If the suspect denies that many times, the interrogator should present a slightly lesser number of times.

"Could it be as few as 900 times?"

If the suspect denies 900 times, the suspect should be asked in a leading manner the number of times that he has used the drug.

"Would it be less than 900 times?"

If the suspect responds affirmatively, the interrogator has obtained a tacit admission of guilt.

"I am sure it would be much less."

The interrogator should then ask the suspect details of his drug use.

"What would be the most number of times that you think that you have tried amphetamines during the last year, being fair to yourself? Could it be as few as 800 times?"

If the suspect states that he is sure it would be less, the interrogator has obtained an initial admission of deception to the polygraph drug question. The suspect should then be asked to give a number that he feels comfortable with as being the truth.

"What would be the total number of times that you feel that you have tried amphetamines without a prescription during the last year?"

The suspect responds, "Probably somewhere between 300 and 400 times."

The interrogator now has the prerogative to confirm the admissions on a subsequent polygraph question.

 "If I were to ask you on the polygraph, during the last year, did you use amphetamines illegally more than 400 times? Would you be truthful if you respond 'no' to that question?"

If the suspect responds positively to the question, the investigator has obtained a post-polygraph admission. This approach could be used on a variety of issues such as the theft of money or merchandise from past employers, undetected crimes, proprietary or classified documents stolen, jobs not listed on the application, etc.

Suggested interrogation themes following a pre-employment polygraph examination:

1. Suggest that most people are too hard on themselves, thinking that they have to be perfect. Suggest that no one is perfect, everyone has made mistakes in life and that your job is simply to seek the truth.

2. Suggest that many people do not tell the entire truth during the polygraph for fear an admission would automatically disqualify them from (the job or continued employment). Further suggest to the subject that it is important to be trusted and that trust can only be accomplished by being truthful and passing the polygraph.

3. If the subject has taken and passed previous polygraph examinations, stress that the subject is a suitable polygraph candidate and compliment the subject for his prior truthfulness. Suggest that the subject has probably made one recent mistake in judgment and now is the time to tell the truth. It can be suggested that the investigator knows the subject is an honorable person based on his prior favorable polygraph test results. It can be further suggested to the subject that by not telling the truth, the investigator can only assume the reason is that the subject is concealing something that is very serious.

4. When a deceptive subject attempts to distort the polygraph recordings by engaging in counter measures (controlled breathing, exerting pressure with his hands or feet, or intentional arm or leg movements during the polygraph examination) it becomes more difficult to determine the specific question the suspect is deceptive on. Following the polygraph examination, the examiner should ask the subject which polygraph test question bothered him the most. There are a few options to this approach. First, if the suspect does admit concern about a specific question, the investigator should inquire as to the reasons

for the suspect's apprehension. If, on the other hand, the suspect denies that any question bothered him, the investigator will have to address each question during the interrogation. The suspect did engage in counter measures to avoid detection.

5. Blame peer pressure, suggesting that someone informed the subject not to admit anything during the polygraph examination. Further suggest that this was obviously wrong advice and confused the subject as to what to do or say during his polygraph examination.

Product Tampering Themes

As a result of the infamous and unsolved 1982 Tylenol product tampering case in which seven people died, product tampering became a federal offense with the passage of the Consumer Tampering Act.

1. Blame the poor security measures taken to ensure the integrity of the product, such as poor packaging, ineffective seals or inappropriate labels making it easy to do

2. Blame the manufacturer for providing a product that did not perform as advertised

3. If the suspect is an employee of the product manufacturer, blame the employer for mistreatment of the employee/offender, contrasting the suspect's motive as just teaching the employer a lesson as opposed to harming an innocent consumer

4. Blame the manufacturer for making exorbitant profits, thus gouging consumers

5. Blame the retailer of the product for some perceived mistreatment of the subject

6. Suggest that the suspect engaged in the behavior to test the system, to see if he could "overcome" the challenges associated

with doing it, or out of sheer boredom

7. Blame alcohol, drugs or stress for causing the offender to act out of character

8. Blame peer pressure, i.e., suggesting that others told the offender the "victim" (retailer or manufacturer) needed to be taught a lesson

9. Blame the media for glamorizing others committing similar acts

10. Minimize the suspect's intent, suggesting it may have been just a "joke" versus trying to put another person in a life-threatening situation

11. Minimize the frequency in which he engaged in tampering activities

12. Suggest that the suspect's intent was not to injure anyone but was economic, to drive down the price of the manufacturer's stock

13. Suggest that the offender did not fully understand the extent of his behavior

14. Suggest that the suspect's intent was to bring to the attention of the public the poor product quality or security of the product

15. Suggest that the offender's intent was simply to call attention to himself (or the faulty security measures) versus trying to hurt someone

16. Suggest that the suspect was just doing what he saw someone else do ("copycat") versus being the person who came up with the original idea

17. Contrast simple extortion or greed versus a more serious motive such as trying to kill someone

18. Contrast an individual acting on his own versus some organized terrorist activity

19. Compliment the offender for never being in trouble before

20. Compliment the offender for being clever, bold or daring

Theme example: Ben works for a candy manufacturer that produces gum with trading cards enclosed. About fifty complaints were received from customers stating that a pornographic picture was included in their trading cards. It is reasonably certain that the obscene photocopied picture appears to have been inserted at the plant where the cards were sealed with the gum. Ben works on the production line where the product is sealed. Employees have been interviewed and Ben's name has surfaced as a disgruntled employee that has had several disputes with management regarding his pay and his constant requests to be put on the day shift. Ben has been interviewed and is believed to have tampered with the trading card packages.

"Ben, our investigation clearly indicates that you did put those pictures of a naked woman inside the trading card packages. Our concern at this point is to find out what caused you to do this. I think it was a combination of several things. First, I know that the company hasn't treated you fairly in what they're paying you. They're making huge profits off of all the employees' hard work and don't offer benefits for the workers. Do they return the favor and reward you with a raise, a new contract or extra compensation? No. Do they even consider your constant requests to get you off of that miserable third shift? No.

"The company takes all of their profits and rewards the executives! They're all given big raises and even bigger bonuses. This treatment makes the hard workers like you angry, upset, and feeling under-appreciated. We've seen some very frustrated employees going off the deep end, walking into work and start blasting with a gun. I'm sure you've read about or seen TV reports of things like that. Ben, you didn't do anything as horrific as that. What you did was less harmful but just as effective in drawing attention to a company that's mistreating its employees.

"Sometimes when we get angry we do things that we normally would never do. We're motivated out of anger because of the way we're mistreated. Some people go to extremes and hurt or kill people. Others like you, Ben, do things that don't hurt people. Ben, I think that this act was the result of a combination of things that caused you to act out of character and put some pictures into the packages. Was this done to close the plant for good or just to vent your frustrations?"

Rape Themes

These themes may also be modified for sexual harassment investigations.

Most rapes are *not* crimes involving sex as the sole motivator, but are rather the result of a combination of motives such as dominance, control, ego gratification, anger, power, revenge and low self-esteem.

The investigator will receive less resistance by having the suspect perceive genuine empathy from the investigator regardless of gender by developing themes that mirror the suspect's justifications. Most rape offenders justify their behavior by blaming the victim for their actions or behavior (such as walking alone late at night, leaving one's residence unsecured, being flirtatious or intoxicated, dressing in a provocative manner, being demeaning toward the suspect, etc.) as causing them to do what they did. Certainly, a myriad of other factors enter into the act that should also be considered during the selection and development of the themes. With this in mind, the most common theme to develop in sexual assaults is to blame the victim for doing something that *provoked* the suspect. The themes suggested do not legally excuse the suspect's behavior but offer moral excuses or psychological justification. Because the victim was jogging late at night or wearing suggestive clothing does not legally justify the crime. During the development of these themes, the interrogator is basically reinforcing the rationalizations that the suspect initially used to justify his behavior.

As an illustration, consider this case. Some time ago, a situation arose in New York following a festive parade on a beautiful day that involved several young men sexually assaulting women as they walked through the group. Many of these men had been drinking during the day and were beginning to get rowdy. As the unsuspecting women walked toward the group, the men began whistling at them and using sexually explicit language. Shortly thereafter, some of the men began to sexually touch the women as they passed. Other men in the crowd saw this occurring and made the decision to join in this behavior. The end result was that several women had been sexually touched and even knocked down.

When conducting an interrogation in a case like this, it would first be necessary to determine what rationalizations occurred causing the suspects to justify their behavior. Knowing that the offenders had consumed alcohol prior to the act, alcohol could be blamed for causing the offenders to act out of character – for clouding their judgment. It could also be suggested that this was more of a situational, spur-of-the-moment decision rather than something that was planned out the night before, thereby minimizing the perceived seriousness of their actions. The suspects could also be told that they were in the wrong place at the wrong time, minimizing the uniqueness of the situation.

Furthermore, contrasting the act of sexually touching the women with the act of actually raping the women may be used to minimize the men's behavior. In addition, the victim's actions, or lack thereof, could further serve as source for psychological blame, i.e., if they (the women) had turned around and walked away this probably would have never happened.

It may also be suggested that the victims were very attractive, wearing revealing clothing and that their behavior may have contributed to the suspect's misinterpreting their intentions. The suspect's behavior may also be psychologically justified by suggesting that everyone else in the group was participating.

The investigator should attempt to select and develop the most appropriate themes based on each sexual assault investigation.

A. Rape themes:

1. Blame the victim's style of dress for leading the suspect on
2. Blame the victim's actions and or behavior, such as
   a. Coming into the suspect's office
   b. Sitting next to the suspect
   c. Inviting the suspect to victim's house
   d. Flirting with the suspect
   e. Allowing the suspect to drive the victim home
   f. Inviting the suspect out on a date
   g. Not securing their residence
   h. Allowing the drapes of the residence to be open
   i. Walking in a dangerous area
   j. Becoming verbally abusive toward the suspect
   k. Telling lies about the suspect
   l. Humiliating the suspect in front of others
   m. Rejecting the suspect's advances
3. Minimize the duration of the incident, contrasting a few minutes versus several hours
4. Blame alcohol or drug usage by the suspect for impairing his judgment
5. Blame peer pressure – one of his buddies talked him into approaching her
6. Blame the suspect's behavior on a gang initiation requirement

7. Blame pornography for providing ideas to the suspect

8. Blame the Internet, suggesting that pornographic sites confuse fantasy with reality

9. Blame the suspect's marital situation for causing him to act out his sexual frustrations (an impending divorce, separation, sexual incompatibility, physical or mental abuse, etc.)

10. Blame differing cultural beliefs, i.e., suggesting that some cultures perceive women to be subservient to a man's needs and desires

11. Blame the victim for being intoxicated, under the influence of drugs or alcohol, or even passing out

12. Blame the suspect's perception of the victim's reputation as being promiscuous

13. Compliment the suspect for not giving the victim a date rape drug

14. Suggest that the suspect did not intend to use force

15. Suggest that the suspect was under stress at the time of the act and wasn't thinking clearly

16. Suggest intent was to show love and affection; however, the situation escalated as a result of a combination of extenuating circumstances, i.e., rejection, humiliation, alcohol, peer pressure, etc.

17. Suggest a combination of medication and alcohol made the suspect act out of character

18. Suggest the suspect may have been mistreated by the opposite sex his entire life, thus blaming women in general

19. Minimize the behavior by suggesting the suspect could have committed a much worse sexual act

Theme example: Peggy, a 28-year-old waitress left her job at 2:00 a.m. As she was approaching her car in the parking lot, a man about her age forced her at gunpoint to engage in sexual intercourse. The incident occurred inside the victim's car. She immediately reported the crime to the authorities and was able to describe a unique tattoo on the offender. Steve, a convicted sexual offender having the exact tattoo, lives in the neighborhood. Eyewitnesses observed Steve at about 1:30 a.m. in the area where Peggy works. Steve is interviewed and is believed to have raped Peggy.

"Steve, there is no doubt that you forced Peggy to engage in sexual intercourse. The reason that I am talking to you is to try to find out exactly why this thing happened. We know that you were drinking that night. Perhaps you had one too many, which can cause people to do things that they otherwise would never do. In any event, your car wasn't working, so you decided to walk home from your local gin mill. As you were walking, you passed the restaurant/bar where Peggy works. You were feeling good and as you cut through the parking lot, you saw Peggy. I spoke to her and I have to admit that she is a very attractive young woman. I think you were attracted to her based on her body language; I mean the way she walked and her attractive dress. In fact, she said that you engaged her in conversation but she ignored you. I think that you began to think that she was being flirtatious and playing hard to get.

"She began to get into her car, but very slowly. I think that you misinterpreted her slow movement as an invitation to join her. Unfortunately, that was not the signal that Peggy wanted to send. You decided to get into the car with her and when she screamed, you panicked. She screamed louder and without thinking, you took the gun out of your pocket, trying to scare her to shut up. Because you had been drinking, I'm thinking your judgment was not exactly perfect. As she struggled, her clothing revealed how attractive she really was. I think that it was at that point that your decision was not based on logic, but on emotion. She resisted and you took offense. You again displayed the gun to quiet her. She only became more threatening. Acting in frustration, you ripped at her dress. She became quiet and you began to think that she had been pretending to resist. She continually said 'no' to your advances, but by now, you misinterpreted them as 'yes.'

"You then had sexual intercourse with Peggy. However, what we need to know, and what is so important, is whether or not the hammer was back on the gun. If the hammer was back, then that tells me that you were going to use the gun. On the other hand, if the hammer was not back, then that tells me that you were just using the gun as a prop. I also think that you were at the wrong place at the wrong time. It's not like you were stalking Peggy and forced her to engage in really deviant things for a long time. In fact, the whole incident took place in less than fifteen minutes. Steve, I'm sure that you will agree with me that this was more of a situational misunderstanding. What I need to know, however, Steve is whether or not the hammer on the gun was back or not when this thing happened. Steve, was the hammer back?"

B. False claim of rape or sexual harassment:

1. Suggest that the false report was made to gain attention, i.e., from spouse, parents, community, school system, etc.
2. Suggest that the false claim was conceived out of poor judgment as a result of being under the influence of drugs, alcohol or stress
3. Suggest that the suspect never thought this false accusation would be investigated to such an extent
4. Suggest that the suspect was previously sexually assaulted, never reported that incident, never obtained the needed psychological counseling and made this accusation with the intent of obtaining such counseling
5. Suggest that the suspect told someone in confidence she was raped and this confidante informed authorities, thereby causing the suspect to maintain the fabricated story

6. Suggest that the false claim was a joke that escalated out of control

7. Contrast what the interrogator believes to be the true intent (attention, revenge, extortion, need for a cover story, becoming pregnant or contracting a social disease) with a much more serious intent, i.e., identifying an individual with the purpose of incarceration

8. Blame someone else for talking the suspect into making this false claim

9. Compliment the suspect for not specifically identifying an individual

10. Minimize the suspect's behavior by suggesting that no one was incarcerated as a result of this behavior

Robbery Themes

A. Blame the victim's actions and behavior:

1. Being in a high crime area

2. Acting in an arrogant manner

3. Leaving money or merchandise unattended

4. Being alone

5. Not walking or talking in a confident manner (making an easy target)

6. Bragging about the amount of money or jewelry they possessed, wearing expensive jewelry, flashing wads of money or numerous credit cards, driving an expensive car, etc.

7. Having poor security, i.e., no surveillance cameras, lack of security personnel, etc.

B. Minimize the seriousness of what the suspect did:

1.   No one was injured
2.   No weapon was used
3.   A weapon was displayed but not used
4.   A weapon was used but the injuries will heal – no one was killed
5.   Blame the victim for not cooperating; the suspect had to use force
6.   Frequency – suggesting one time versus several times; once a month versus every day
7.   Contrasting acting on impulse versus premeditation
8.   Suggest that the suspect believed the victim could afford the loss
9.   The suspect's intent was to provide for life's necessities versus getting money to buy drugs
10. Minimize the dollar amount/value of the items that were stolen

C. Blame outside factors for causing the suspect to commit the act:

1.   Alcohol or drugs – acted out of character
2.   Unemployment – no income
3.   Peer pressure – the idea was suggested to him
4.   Life circumstances – because of his criminal record he cannot obtain a job
5.   Gang initiation

Theme example: Lindsey observed a jewelry salesman displaying his $250,000 in jewelry from his briefcase to a perspective client at the concierge lounge of an exclusive hotel. Lindsey later robbed the salesman at gunpoint. Informants identified Lindsey as the perpetrator.

"Lindsey, we know that you were in the lounge when that salesman was displaying his jewelry. We also know that later that night you pointed a gun at him to turn over the briefcase. What I think caused this to happen was the fact that the salesman was flashing all of his jewelry in plain sight. Had he not done that, you wouldn't be here right now. He got careless, violated proper security procedures and we know what resulted. He has been selling jewelry for more than twenty years and should have known better. It is my understanding that the jewelry is insured so that his employer is not going to be out any money. One huge positive in this situation is that no one was injured or more importantly, killed. If you had pulled the trigger, we'd be dealing with a totally different situation. Lindsey, the jewelry can always be replaced.

"Not too long ago I had another very similar situation in which the victim resisted during a robbery and during the subsequent struggle the gun went off, killing the guy. That situation escalated to a homicide, which is a lot different than stealing something. That guy can't bring back the person's life. Our concern is whether or not you would have used the gun had the salesman resisted. Were you going to shoot him if he resisted or was the gun just used as a prop? There is a difference between murder, attempted murder and theft. That is what I'd like to resolve here. The question is not if you took the jewelry, but what force you had intended to use. Were your intentions to shoot and kill the salesman?"

Sabotage Themes

These themes primarily apply to employee sabotage but can be modified to apply to criminal damage to property by non-employees.

A. Blame the victim's (employer's) actions and behavior by:

1. Not promoting the suspect or promoting less qualified individuals
2. Not recognizing the suspect's dedication and hard work
3. Not being appreciative of the suspect's extra efforts

4. Forcing the suspect to constantly work under crisis conditions
5. Reducing work hours or overtime pay
6. Creating a stressful work environment due to constant negative rumors (lay-offs, pay cuts, benefit cuts, possible transfers, etc.)
7. Forcing the suspect to work in a substandard or hazardous work environment
8. Failing to meet union demands or to allow open negotiations

B. Blame outside factors:

1. Peer pressure, stress, alcohol or drugs
2. The thrill, excitement and challenge of trying to get away with it
3. Emotions such as anger, frustration, revenge, etc.
4. The media – suggesting that this was a copycat action versus original idea

C. Minimization themes:

1. Contrast property damage versus human injury
2. Contrast minor bodily injury versus death
3. Contrast doing it one time versus many times
4. Contrast spur-of-the-moment act versus premeditated
5. Contrast doing it as a joke versus a malicious act designed to hurt someone
6. Suggest that the suspect's intent was to bring attention to a problem, not to cause the extensive amount of damage that resulted
7. Suggest that the suspect's intent was to show potential security or safety flaws
8. Suggest that the suspect's intent was merely to get attention; his real intent was not to commit the offense but rather be discovered

Theme example: Shortly after take-off, a helicopter was forced to make an emergency landing; fortunately, no one was injured. It was discovered that a hydraulic line was cut, causing the fluid to slowly leak out while under pressure. Subsequently, two other helicopters were discovered to have had their hydraulics cut in the same manner. Ben is suspected of committing the act of sabotage because his military tour of duty has been extended well beyond what was initially projected.

"Ben, our investigation indicated that you caused those cuts in the hydraulic lines of those three helicopters. Whenever we do get involved in a situation like this, the first thing we do is a thorough investigation. Could this have been an accident, a defect or an intentional act? We have reviewed videos, taken fingerprints, conducted extensive interviews; we have exhausted everything humanly possible and everything indicates that you intentionally cut those lines.

"As you may have heard, tampering with aircraft safety devices, weapons or other types of vehicles is very common among the services. Fortunately, most of the acts that are deliberately done do not result in physical injury. However, some acts do either cause serious injury or even worse, death. I remember talking to one individual that was tampering with parachutes that ultimately resulted in the death of several innocent people. I also know of another fellow who threw bolts into jet aircraft engines that caused some very severe explosions. One of those explosions caused the death of the pilot and copilot. My point here with you, Ben, is first, no one was injured, and in fact no choppers were severely damaged.

"The most important thing right now, Ben, is to determine what caused you to act out of character and do something like this. I think it was a combination of factors that caused you to cut those lines. Foremost is the fact that you're ready to be sent home, you've done your tour, you've endured a lot of hardships and you find out that you're going to be here another six months to a year; a second tour of duty! These pilots are being rotated out of here quicker than anyone.   In fact, I've had many complaints from people like you about the sarcasm of the pilots saying that they'll be home safe and sound after only one tour of duty. The more you hear these wisecracks from the pilots, the more depressed and angry you become.

"Ben, you knew that there was a backup hydraulic system. You also knew that the slow leakage of fluid wouldn't cause a crash, but you knew it would get someone's attention. I think that this was done to get even with the pilots that were riding you and perhaps show them that they're no better than anyone else. In fact, I'm thinking that maybe you were going to bring the cut hydraulic lines to someone's attention before anything happened. I think that you simply wanted the recognition that you've never been given, perhaps with the intention of getting out of here sooner.

"Ben, did you cut those hydraulic lines to hurt or kill someone or was it just because you were stressed out as a result of your extended tour and the pilots constantly riding you? I think it was because of their treatment and the stress of having to stay here and not being with your family! Is that what caused you to do this?"

Shoplifting Themes

A. Adults:

1. Blame the economy for causing consumer prices to escalate to an unreasonable level
2. Blame the fact that the elderly have to live on a fixed income and

don't have any money for discretionary spending

3. Blame the store for high markups

4. Blame the store for long checkout lines, not providing adequate help, suggesting that the suspect acted out of frustration

5. Blame a recent stressful event (such as loss of job, health issues, death of a loved one, etc) for causing the suspect's uncharacteristic behavior

6. Suggest the suspect's behavior began innocently i.e., his child playing with a toy from the store, the cashier failing to charge for the item and the suspect's behavior escalating into similar intentional thefts and ultimately resulting in an uncontrollable addictive behavior

7. Suggest that the suspect could not live within his limited budget

8. Suggest that the suspect was too embarrassed to purchase the item

9. Suggest that the suspect had consumed alcohol, wasn't thinking clearly and acted out of character

10. Suggest that the suspect did not have enough money at the time so he acted on the spur-of-the-moment – it was not a premeditated act

11. Suggest that the suspect forgot his money and needed the item right away, suggesting that perhaps the suspect was planning to return at a later time to pay for the item

12. Suggest that the store mistreated the suspect on previous occasions by overcharging him, failing to put all of his items in the shopping bag after his purchase so that the suspect paid for something he never received, not properly marking down sale items, treating him in a rude and abrasive manner, etc.

13. Contrast shoplifting with much more serious crimes such as armed robbery, rape, etc.

14. Suggest that the suspect's intent was to personally use the item as opposed to selling the item

15. Minimize the value of the item or the frequency of the shoplifting

B. Juveniles:

1. Blame the age of the offender, suggesting that younger people are expected to make mistakes
2. Blame peer pressure – one of his buddies talked him into it (bragging rights or just showing off); suggest that the suspect was dared or challenged
3. Blame the lack of store security for creating such an opportunity
4. Blame the store for placing tempting products outside the store or near an exit
5. Blame the suspect's parents for not providing a realistic allowance
6. Blame the suspect's parents for not allowing the suspect to have a job so that he can earn some spending money
7. Blame the suspect's age for not allowing him to get a job so that he could earn spending money
8. Blame the store for mistreating the suspect on a prior occasion, suggesting that the suspect's behavior was just an attempt to balance the scale
9. Suggest that the act was committed for the thrill or excitement of doing it
10. Suggest that the act was part of a gang initiation rite
11. Suggest that the suspect was too embarrassed to purchase the item
12. Suggest that the suspect was not old enough to purchase the item
13. Suggest that the suspect took the item for a friend who could not afford to buy it
14. Suggest that the suspect could not afford an item that everyone else owned
15. Contrast shoplifting with a more serious crime such as armed robbery, rape, etc.
16. Contrast doing it one time versus several times
17. Minimize the value of the item(s) involved

18. Minimize the theft by suggesting the store could afford the loss

Theme example: Cindy is observed by store security suspiciously reaching inside her jacket. They then observed Cindy leave the store at which time the security alarm is activated. Security approaches, Cindy runs and is thought to have tossed something into the trash. Five DVDs from the store were recovered from the trashcan. She is questioned by security, denies shoplifting the DVDs as well as throwing anything into the trash. She said other people were leaving the store when the alarm sounded and said she ran because other people were running.

"Cindy, our investigation indicates that you took the five DVDs from the store. Our concern is the reason why you did this. Let me explain to you, Cindy, why people take things like this. Most people take things that they can't afford or don't have the time to return and purchase because they didn't bring enough money. In other words, it's a combination of convenience and lack of money. The price the store was charging for the DVDs was pretty high. You probably know that other stores are selling the same DVDs for a much lower price. I'm not saying that this makes things right, but sometimes when we want something and feel we're being cheated, we may do something out of anger – like taking the items. I'm beginning to think this is not your lifestyle to take things from stores without permission. I'm thinking that this was probably an isolated incident.

"The other reason people take things from stores without paying is because it is their lifestyle. Some people steal things not for lack of money, but with the intent to sell the stuff to get some money for other things like drugs, alcohol or gambling. I don't think this was your reason. I also don't think you have a history of shoplifting. I think this was a one-time deal in which you acted out of impulse. In fact, the store was crowded and the checkout lines were ten to fifteen people deep! The store should have had extra cashiers so as to expedite the shoppers. I also think that you were frustrated and made an impulsive decision. If you were a dishonest person, you would have taken fifty DVDs. You didn't take fifty. You only took the ones that you wanted and couldn't afford. My concern, Cindy, is this just the first time you did something like this at the store or have you done this hundreds of times? Cindy, this was just the first time, wasn't it?"

Smuggling/Customs Themes

These themes are primarily directed toward individuals attempting to bring contraband into the United States. Common items smuggled consist of illegal drugs, non-approved drugs, currency, exotic animals and counterfeit items such as clothes, watches, handbags, CDs, DVDs, etc. Themes will also address the issue of smuggling people into the country.

A. General Themes:

1. Blame the bureaucracy for making it so difficult to obtain the proper licenses to import items such as protected wildlife or property

2. Blame the laws, rules, regulations and policies as being unfair, unrealistic or outdated

3. Blame the economics of supply and demand, suggesting that the suspect was just meeting the market's needs

4. Blame the lucrative monetary offer for the "goods" as being too tempting to resist, particularly given the suspect's difficult financial circumstances

5. Blame the government/country for trying to maintain a monopoly on these goods

6. Blame the suspect's poor economic situation as causing him to

make this mistake in judgment, for causing him to do something out of desperation

7. Blame the high prices of the products; the suspect was merely offering an alternative "knockoff"

8. Suggest that the suspect was simply doing someone a favor

9. Suggest that the items (for example, Cuban cigars) were for personal use or enjoyment as opposed to selling them for an exorbitant profit

10. Suggest that the suspect's intent for bringing in the items (such as rare or exotic animals) was simply to gain bragging rights or to show off versus selling them for profit

11. Suggest that the act was the result of a dare made by someone

12. Suggest that the suspect's intent was simply to see if it could be done – a personal challenge

13. Suggest that the suspect's intent was to test the security, i.e., a challenge

14. Suggest that the suspect's intent was simply to avoid paying taxes or to pay less for the items if purchased in his own country

15. Suggest that the items involved were not hazardous or dangerous

16. Suggest that it was someone else's idea and the suspect simply went along with their plan as opposed to developing the idea himself

17. Contrast smuggling with more serious crimes such as child molestation or murder

18. Minimize the frequency of the activity

19. Minimize the duration of the events

B. Smuggling people:

1. Suggest that the suspect's intent was to reunite family members

2. Suggest that the suspect was doing them a favor

3. Suggest that the individuals could have gained entry but could not

wait for their legal paperwork to be processed

4. Suggest that the victim (smuggled individuals) approached the suspect as opposed to the suspect trying to recruit individuals
5. Suggest the suspect believed the government expects a certain amount of smuggling; in fact, alien restrictions will soon become less limiting
6. Compliment the suspect for wanting to provide a better lifestyle for the illegal aliens
7. Minimize the frequency with which he engaged in such activity
8. Blame the government's unfair and unjust restrictive policies
9. Blame the bureaucratic red tape in obtaining the proper paperwork for legal entry
10. Compliment the suspect on the fact that no one was hurt or injured
11. Contrast a humanitarian act versus trafficking in human slavery

Theme example: Our investigation reveals that Reggie has been bringing counterfeit handbags and watches into the U.S to be sold on the street.

"Reggie, we know that you have been bringing imitation handbags and watches into the U.S. I think that there are several reasons why you are doing this. The most common reason is the easy money it brings you. The people that buy these things from you know that they're knockoffs, so you're not cheating or deceiving anyone. Secondly, the people who are buying the watches and handbags cannot afford to purchase the real thing so you are not depriving the real manufacturer of any money. In fact, one way to look at it is that you are providing advertisement for the real product. The more people that see the product, the more they want it and those that can afford it are not going to be happy with an imitation anyway. These people you sold to couldn't afford to buy the real thing anyway. It's a win-win situation.

"You're making some money selling the imitations, the people buying it know it's not the real thing and they are happy and like to show off and let people think it's real. The manufacturer of the genuine items isn't being deprived of anything because these people who buy from you couldn't afford and wouldn't buy the real thing because it's too expensive anyway. My concern, Reggie, is are you telling people when they buy your stuff that it's a good copy or imitation or are you cheating them by telling them it's the real thing and you are selling it at such a low price because it's stolen?"

Stalking Themes

Stalking is generally considered the persistent, distressing or threatening behavior consisting of at least two elements: 1) the suspect must repeatedly follow the victim and 2) must engage in conduct that annoys or alarms the victim and serves no legitimate purpose.

A. Minimize the suspect's intent and/or blame outside factors:

1. Suggest that the suspect's intent was to take photos or videos for personal use versus trying to sell them or blackmail the victim
2. Suggest that the suspect cannot help himself – that his behavior is an addiction that requires professional help
3. Suggest that the suspect never trespassed on private property but only uses public venues
4. Suggest that the act was a personal challenge
5. Suggest that the suspect's intent was actually to protect the victim
6. Suggest that others have successfully engaged in similar behavior
7. Suggest that the act was the fulfillment of an uncontrollable fantasy
8. Blame alcohol, drugs or peer pressure for causing the suspect to

exercise poor judgment

9. Blame the media or the Internet for depicting the victim as unique or being very approachable
10. Blame the media for the glamorizing of other stalkers
11. Minimize the frequency of the act
12. Contrast the suspect's intent as acting out of love or affection versus trying to do something malicious

B. Suggest that the suspect did this because the victim:

1. Engaged in flirtatious behavior
2. Wore provocative clothing
3. Previously was demeaning to the suspect
4. Reminded the offender of someone he reveres or loves
5. Was so easily approachable
6. Was so easily accessible
7. Was such a positive role model
8. Had very poor security
9. Misled the offender through their words or actions
10. Had a very identifiable license plate, boat or residence
11. Was very popular; everyone wanted to be near him/her

Theme example: Joe is accused of stalking Jay, a prominent local sports figure.

"Joe, we know that you have been following Jay over the last four weeks – you were spotted outside his house as well as following his car. Our concern, is what were your intentions? Some people do things like this just as a challenge or fantasy; others do it because they intend to eventually harm that person or his family.

"Joe, I'm not saying that you were planning on abducting Jay or his family and holding them for ransom.   I think that you were simply influenced by his status and charisma and were simply working up the courage to actually talk to him with the intent of wanting to be friends.

"Sometimes people just can't help themselves from following someone like Jay. Slowly and without even knowing it, it turns into an obsession or uncontrollable urge. It's very similar to watching your favorite TV program. Certain TV stars mesmerize some viewers and nothing is more important in their lives than watching their favorite TV actor. This is obviously compulsive behavior, but harmless behavior. Most of those viewers are normal people behaving out of admiration. I'm sure you know what I'm talking about. However, some people don't have such a positive motivation; their intent is to be harmful. You see, Joe, that is why we're talking to you today. Were you following Jay just to get to know him and tell him how much you admired him or were your intentions to harm him? I think it was just admiration, right?"

Stolen Property Themes

A. Receiving Stolen Property:

1. Blame the "deal" as being too good to pass up
2. Blame the dealer for approaching the suspect
3. Blame peer pressure
4. Blame need versus greed
5. Blame the effect of stress – the constant need to provide essential items or gifts for family
6. Suggest that the purchase was a spur-of-the-moment decision versus something that was premeditated
7. Suggest that the purchaser could not afford the retail price
8. Suggest that everyone has done this kind of thing before

9. Minimize the value of the goods involved or the frequency of the purchases
10. Contrast buying innocuous stolen property with the purchase of more serious items such as drugs, guns, child pornography, etc.

B. Selling Stolen Property:

1. Contrast the suspect being solicited to buy the items as opposed to initiating the contact and approaching the seller
2. Contrast selling stolen property as an act that simply supplements the suspect's income as opposed to an activity that is the sole source of income for the suspect
3. Contrast stealing merchandise versus just selling the merchandise
4. Suggest that the suspect was threatened (for example, that the authorities would be informed) if he did not sell the property in question
5. Suggest that the suspect was doing a favor for someone who could not afford to pay the retail cost for the property
6. Suggest that the suspect could not get a decent paying job and was forced to engage in this type of activity
7. Suggest that the suspect's living expenses increased at a rate that was significantly greater than his work-related income
8. Blame the need for additional income
9. Blame the economy
10. Minimize the frequency of the activity or the value of the merchandise being sold

Theme example: Dennis is a pawnshop dealer accused of purchasing and selling stolen jewelry.

"Dennis, we know that you knew the jewelry was stolen when you bought it from Cindy. Our concern is whether or not you are telling people like

Cindy to go out and steal stuff so that you can resell it, or if they're doing it on their own because they know that you'll give them a fair price. First of all, who got hurt here? The people that Cindy stole the jewelry from probably had it insured and in all probability insured for more than the replacement value! I doubt that they're losing any money. I'm not saying it's right to do this but no one was killed or raped or anything like that.

"Dennis, the woman that you bought the jewelry from has a tough life; she's got a 'Jones' for cocaine, has kids that have to eat and need a place to live. You're not a cold-hearted person who wants to see people suffer. In fact, you probably thought that you were doing her a favor by buying the jewelry. You gave Cindy a fair price and now you're out the money. You need to make a living. You're not getting rich off this. I don't see you driving a Mercedes and living in Beverly Hills! Someone comes into your shop, sees the jewelry, decides that they want it and you sell it to break even or just to get it out of your shop. My concern is, did you buy the jewelry to help Cindy out or did you tell Cindy to rip off this specific piece of jewelry?"

Terrorist Themes

"Let every nation know, whether it wishes us well or ill, that we shall pay any price, bear any burden, meet any hardship, support any friend, oppose any foe to assure the survival and success of liberty."

John F. Kennedy (1917-1963)
35th U.S. President

The author and Daniel S. Malloy, Seminar Director of John E. Reid and Associates developed the following terrorist interrogation themes immediately following the abhorrent 9/11 attacks. They were designed and intended to serve as a guide for the investigator and need to be selected or modified depending on the specific circumstance of the crime. Examples: organized group versus individual act, single incident, loss of life, loss of property, etc. Subsequently, additional interrogation tactics with respect to guerrilla warfare and terrorist motives were added by staff member William P. Schrieber, based on his post-9/11 training experiences in Baghdad.

Motivations of a Terrorist Group (both of its leaders and members)

1. Pursuit of a just cause:

- Religious
- Political agenda or differences
- Social/Cultural
- Economic
- Protection of family and country

2. Revenge/retaliation – resulting from violent encounters with the victim:

- Financial – unemployed or not able to provide an adequate standard of living
- Fear – retaliation from others for not joining the group
- Social alienation – therefore proving self-worth
- Boredom – seeking attention

Primary Terrorist Interrogation Themes:

1. Suggest that the suspect was offered money or something of value, such as food, clothing, shelter, medical supplies, medical treatment for family, etc. that he desperately needed in exchange for committing a terrorist act

2. Suggest that the suspect's intent was designed to correct a wrongdoing or unjust behavior by the victim

3. Suggest that the suspect's behavior was based on sound, fundamental religious teachings versus personal opinions or beliefs

4. Suggest that the action was taken to bring attention to a very serious problem

5. Blame the victim for

   a. Being non-responsive to past problems

      Example: "The U.S. favors other governments and ignores aid to countries that really need help. You wanted people to become aware of this prejudice and force this government to change its policies. Governments like the U.S. do not immediately respond to diplomatic discussions."

   b. Taking so long to change policies (if they are ever changed at all)

      Example: "While people talk and debate, your people are needlessly suffering and dying. Talk does not feed or protect your children. You want action now. Sometimes the only way to change a wrong to a right is to become aggressive."

   c. Being too militarily and economically powerful

      Example: "Sometimes people that have everything lose touch with reality. They don't know what it's like to go without food, water, medical aid or shelter. Instead of acting in the best interest of the people, they act in their best interest. Why? Because who is going to challenge them? No one will make a challenge simply due to fear of the military or economic power. However, you realized that you needed to protect your values despite the threatening power."

   d. Engaging in policies of economically or militarily assisting hostile countries or individuals (which could be construed as terrorism in reverse)

Example: Depending on how westernized the suspect is to U.S. culture or movies, the following dialog may be appropriate. "If you ever have seen the movie *Braveheart*, you know that the viewer begins to side with William Wallace, the main character of the movie, portrayed by Mel Gibson, who is protecting his country, Scotland to the death. In fact, William Wallace so prophetically said, 'Men don't follow titles; they follow courage.' Wallace was the symbol of courage and passion that men followed, protecting his land from invaders from England. He does this by organizing sympathizers to not only fight, but also prepare to give their lives for freedom. A great many people did die. Most every person, including myself, understood and cheered for the protectors of their country. I had to ask myself, who were the aggressors, the terrorists? Who were the innocent victims? People sometimes have their views or perspectives swayed by the media as to the real truth. If your true intent was designed to show the courage and passion that others could follow, as well as to educate people as to the truth of the situation, and what you did was not done as an act of revenge or retaliation, then that needs to be known. This was done to educate, wasn't it?"

e. Being insensitive or oppressive

Example: "I know you have tried to make the U.S. understand that it has no business in your country's affairs but the U.S. just would not listen and needed a 'wake-up call' to keep out of the affairs of other countries."

f. Focusing on economic interests versus humanitarian interests

6. Minimize the repercussions, consequences and/or motives of the suspect's tactics

a. The financial loss of the act could have been much greater

b. The loss of life was minimal and could have been much worse

c. Those injured or killed were soldiers or diplomats, not children

d. Those injured or killed were fanatics and deserved what they got

e. The injuries were not that serious

f. The number of incidents were limited (one time versus many; ten times versus hundreds of times)

f. The limited duration of the event (one day versus one week; one month versus one year)

g. Suggest that several warnings were given versus no warnings being given

h. Suggest that the suspect's original intent was not to harm anyone

i. Suggest that the suspect acted out of uncontrolled anger – acted without thinking

j. Suggest that the suspect acted out of desperation – he saw that nothing else was working

k. Suggest that not all acts are the responsibility of "terrorists" but rather individuals who are just acting as a "copycat"

l. Imply that the suspect's intent was to claim freedom for future generations

m. Imply that the suspect's intent was to bring attention to a serious problem versus trying to start a war

7. Blame U.S. politicians for self-serving interests and caving in to making decisions that are monetarily or politically motivated, becoming nothing more than puppets to big interest groups

8. Compliment the suspect for being bold, clever and/or daring
   Example: "Someone like you has to take the risk for freedom for

your people and your beliefs and I think that is what has caused you to act this way. You and your actions here are an example to the world of your dedication to a belief, and a warning to others to stay out of people's business. Talk is cheap. People pay attention to action and this is not a time to be diplomatic. Your actions are designed to cause an immediate reaction for the world to take notice. Your actions demonstrate your courage and true conviction."

9. Suggest that the intent of the act was humanitarian versus criminal

10. Suggest or imply that there is strong evidence that implicates the suspect

11. Suggest that the suspect acted on impulse versus premeditation

12. Suggest that the suspect acted to experience the thrill and excitement of the act

13. Blame the suspect's desperate financial circumstances and the country's failing economy for causing him to get involved in this type of activity

14. Suggest that the commission of the crime was out of character for the suspect

15. Suggest that the suspect was forced to act with "terrorists" for fear of retaliation to him or his family

16. Suggest that the suspect was misled by "terrorists" regarding the seriousness of the acts

17. Play one against the other by suggesting and/or implying the suspected accomplice is telling the truth and cooperating with authorities

Example: "We are going to believe who talks first. By saying nothing, it will appear to everyone that this was your idea, that you were the mastermind. Right now others might be saying that this was all your idea, that you recruited them, that you threatened them and if they did not go along with what you wanted, something would happen to them or their families. Now this is your opportunity to explain your side of what happened before others start telling lies about you."

18. Blame poor security or controls

Example: "The U.S. (victims) lacks proper control and security, making it easy to commit such acts. If there had been tighter controls and security at the (airports, train station, bridges, etc.) and better-trained security professionals, these events probably would never have happened. Our lax attitudes make it simple to do."

19. Blame the media for being biased and not reporting the news fairly

20. As a last resort, develop themes suggesting that the suspect may not be a terrorist but rather a copycat offender or even an individual playing a joke. If the suspect is actually a terrorist, developing these themes might make it easier for the perpetrator to confess, believing that he has deceived the interrogator. Furthermore, if the suspect was truly not a terrorist but rather a copycat offender or even an individual playing a joke, these themes will now appear even more meaningful and make it easier to admit to the act of wrongdoing.

Copycat Terrorist Themes:

1. Contrast someone just acting as a "copycat" versus an actual terrorist

2. Suggest that the suspect's intent was to commit the act as a joke versus actually trying to harm someone

3. Suggest that the suspect's intent was to impress others so that he would be accepted into their group

4. Contrast the copycat offender that did not inflict serious injury

versus the zealous terrorist that has inflicted serious injury

5. Contrast the fact that the suspect just engaged in verbal threats versus physical threats

6. Contrast the limited impact of a single individual (copycat) acting alone versus the damage caused by an organized militia group

7. Suggest that the misfortune in the suspect's life (being unemployed, disgruntled, divorced, financially burdened, bored, etc.), caused the uncharacteristic behavior

8. Blame the government for being too intrusive, insensitive, etc., and that the suspect was just trying to bring attention to the issue

9. Blame peer pressure

10. Blame stress, alcohol or drugs for clouding the suspect's judgment

Hoax Terrorist Themes:

Another area of terrorist investigations would be hoaxes, either false threats or threats not carried out. Many of these offenders are powerless people seeking excitement and the perception of importance, viewing the situation as a means of compensating for their shortcomings.

1. Suggest that the suspect's intent was to call attention to the lack of preparedness of the government to deal with actual terrorist threats

2. Suggest that the suspect's intent was just to "test" the system, to confirm that the system was prepared to address a real terrorist attack

3. Blame the stress and pressure that the suspect was under from home, family or his job, which caused him to act out of character Example: "Sometimes because of outside influences we all do things that when we think back, we know were out of character. We would never have done or said such things had it not been for

some outside influence. There sometimes is no good reason or explanation for why we did something. It was just plain dumb! When we did something or said something out of character, it probably was because we were just not thinking clearly. Everybody does things without thinking. Is that what happened here? I tend to think you just were not thinking clearly when you did this. Isn't that the case? You didn't mean to hurt anyone, did you?"

4. Suggest that the suspect was only joking versus actually intending to carry out the offense

5. Blame the victim for engaging in some prior action or behavior that was offensive, humiliating or degrading toward the suspect

6. Suggest that the suspect made the veiled threat simply to accomplish or fulfill a need, such as breaking an appointment in bankruptcy court, getting out of taking a test, getting out of work, etc.

7. In cases involving the discovering of a fake terrorist letter, fake biochemical element, etc., suggest that the suspect's motive was simply to gain attention; contrast the true motive of attention with something much more serious

8. Suggest that the suspect was acting under the influence of alcohol or drugs, clouding his judgment

9. Suggest that the suspect was caught up in the euphoria or excitement of the situation and acted without thinking

Themes for Obtaining Knowledge of Terrorist Activity:

If the suspect resists confessing to direct involvement in terrorist activity, the interrogator may pursue the option that the individual is harboring knowledge about others who are involved in such activity. Explain to the suspect that you would like to believe that he is not directly involved or responsible for what happened. Therefore, suggest to the suspect that if he is not directly involved in the terrorist act and only has knowledge, it is critical to explain this.

1. Minimize the seriousness of the offense in which the suspect is concealing knowledge
   Example: Contrast the situation in which there is the disbursement of low-grade anthrax in which no one was seriously injured versus the situation in which smallpox is released (which is extremely contagious and fatal with little or no treatment available)
2. Suggest that by disclosing the names of individuals involved the suspect is demonstrating his cooperation and helping to establish the fact that he is not directly involved
3. Suggest limited confidentiality – explain to the suspect that you are not going to tell other suspects what he tells you
4. Contrast a situation in which the suspect learns the identity of the perpetrators after the fact versus the situation in which the suspect has guilty knowledge in advance
5. If the suspect is reluctant to provide names of the offenders, have the suspect provide a physical description, unique identifying body parts or unusual clothing/jewelry (tattoos, missing limbs, limp, stutter, raspy voice, nicknames, etc.)
6. Obtain identities of friends or neighbors of the terrorist with the intent ofdetermining his general geographic location

Guerrilla Warfare Interrogation Themes:

1. Firing RPG (rocket-propelled grenade) rounds, mortar fire or small arms fire at troops, civilians, aircraft or vehicles
   a. The suspect's intent was to scare people, not to kill anyone
   b. The suspect was given or promised money to survive and/or provide for his family if he did this

    c. Blame the victim (U.S.) for spreading values not consistent with the suspect's culture

    d. Blame others for threatening the suspect with retribution to himself, family or friends if he didn't do this

    e. Suggest that the suspect was just following orders

    f. Suggest that the suspect acted out of blind rage, hopelessness or even boredom

    g. Suggest that the suspect was acting to protect his family from harm

    h. Suggest that the suspect was a passive supporter or sympathizer versus a violent fanatic

    i. Suggest that the suspect did this only on one occasion versus doing it all of the time – that he did it as a spur-of-the-moment act versus a premeditated act

2. Harboring terrorists in home and/or operating a safe house

    a. Suggest that the suspect was simply doing a favor for friends

    b. Suggest that the suspect offered his home in return for money that he was promised (money to be used to help his family survive)

    c. Suggest that the suspect did not know the individuals were terrorists

    d. Suggest that the suspect was simply being a good neighbor and keeping with religious, political or cultural values

    e. Suggest that the suspect offered safe harbor out of fear of retribution to self, family or friends if he did not cooperate with the terrorists

    f. Suggest that the suspect was just following orders

3. Planting improvised explosive devices designed to kill and injure troops or sympathetic civilians

    a. Blame the troops or sympathetic civilians for being in an area where they didn't belong

    b. Suggest that the suspect's intent was to injure but not to kill anyone

c. Suggest that the suspect acted out of fear of retribution to self, family or friends if he did not cooperate with the terrorists

d. Suggest that the suspect planted the device in return for money that he was promised (money to be used to help his family survive)

e. Blame someone else for talking the suspect into planting the device

f. Suggest that the suspect did this because his religious, political or social values were being threatened

g. Suggest that the suspect did this to challenge or test the security measures that were in place

h. Suggest that the suspect's intent was to act as a warning to the troops (or sympathetic civilians) so as to prevent escalation of further aggression

i. Suggest that the suspect's intent was to seek accurate media attention to expose the troops as being the aggressors

Third Person Themes

Third person themes focus on telling the offender a story or a series of stories about others that have committed similar but more serious crimes. These stories can be real or fictitious. The moral of the story should be to demonstrate that the interrogator knows from personal experience that good people make mistakes in judgment. These third person themes are similar to crimes that the suspect has committed. Examples of similar crimes can be taken from the media, a similar case the investigator was involved in or a story regarding how the interrogator could have conceivably acted in a similar hypothetical situation.

These themes are most successful when confronting a hostile offender or if the offender has a representative in the interrogation room. If interrogating a juvenile with a parent present, a criminal suspect with an attorney present, or an employee with a union representative present, third person themes should become the primary interrogational approach. The purpose of developing third person themes in these situations is that the theme does not directly attack the offender's actions or behavior and therefore does not attack the offender's representative. In fact, the third person themes should periodically be directed to the offender's representative. The suspect's representative will more likely listen to the interrogator since this approach is not attacking the suspect. The suspect, in turn, will observe the representative listening attentively to the interrogator. This will generally cause the offender to mirror his representative, to listen and become less aggressive.

The purpose of developing one or more third person themes is to show the suspect and his representative that other people have committed similar crimes. It will therefore be suggested via these examples that the suspect's crime is not unique in any way. Simultaneously, by projecting a series of more serious third person themes, the offender and the representative will begin to realize that the crime committed could have been much more serious or reprehensible. The overall impact of third person themes is to not only minimize the uniqueness or perception of the seriousness of the crime to the suspect, but also to the suspect's representative. The interrogator may present alternatives to the suspect as soon as the representative quiets and begins showing interest.

The offender's representative should be seated next to but slightly behind the offender. The interrogator should be seated directly in front of the offender. This positioning makes it easier for the interrogator to direct third person themes to both the offender and his representative. This arrangement will also make it more difficult for the suspect to seek assistance from the representative.

Scenario 1

Ed, a 17-year-old high school senior, vandalizes his ex-girlfriend Elaine's car by scratching it with a key on three separate occasions while it was parked at the high school parking lot. The offender's parent is present during the interrogation. No one was injured and the cost to repair the damage is about $500.

"Ed and Mr. Jones (his parent), our investigation indicates that Ed did cause those scratches to the red Mustang while it was parked in the high school parking lot. First, let me say that we all make mistakes in life. I can think back when I was in high school many years ago. I made decisions back then that I wouldn't even consider today. Once I was with a buddy in his car as a railroad gate was going down. What did we do? We raced under the gates. Only problem was that the car stalled while on the tracks. We had to get out and push the car out of the way of the oncoming train. Not too smart, right? Today, I wouldn't even think of doing something that stupid.

"I also remember a friend of mine being dumped by his girlfriend. He was angry so he kept calling her late at night and hanging up. He made these nuisance phone calls for a month. The problem was that the mother of his girlfriend thought someone was stalking her and she had the phone company put a lock on the phone, which registered each call made to the phone number. Back then we didn't have caller ID. Anyway, the police found out that my best friend was making these harassing calls. They were concerned if my buddy was going to physically harm his ex-girlfriend or her mother. There was serious concern that this situation may have escalated to something more serious than just nuisance phone calls. It wasn't until they talked to my friend that they were assured this was just meant to be a nuisance with no intent to harm anyone. In fact, it was the result of my buddy being hurt because his girlfriend dumped him for one of his best friends. He cared very deeply for her.

"It's for this reason that I am talking to you. You see, Ed, the issue here is not whether you caused those scratches to Elaine's car, but rather why. And I think you were just like this other student who didn't consider the ramifications of his actions. He acted out of emotion and frustration just like you. Fortunately, in your situation, no one was hurt and the damage can always be repaired. If Elaine or her mom had been hurt, I think you would agree with me that this would be an entirely different situation. Wouldn't you? (Ed nods).

"Good, Ed. Let's get this cleared up. I don't think you wanted to hurt anyone, did you? I'm sure you didn't. I think you were simply acting out of frustration and poor judgment, right? I further think that if you could live that day over again, things would be different. Am I right? You were just acting out of frustration, right?"

Scenario 2

Carm broke into a house on Walter Lane, stealing about $5,000 in jewelry. An informant identified him to the authorities. Carm was interviewed and will be interrogated with his attorney, Mr. Mullen, present. As in the previous scenario, the seating arrangements should be the same. The interrogator should not be intimidated by the presence of the suspect's attorney, but rather view this situation not as an exercise in futility but one that allows an opportunity for a confession. Had the suspect's attorney refused to cooperate and not allow the interrogator to confront his client, the opportunity to obtain a confession would be nonexistent.

In this case, particularly if the suspect was read his Miranda rights, the interrogator's approach should primarily address third person themes. Third person interrogation themes do not directly attack the suspect or his attorney but rather illustrate that other individuals have committed similar but more serious offenses. The investigator should direct the third person themes to both the suspect and his attorney. As the attorney begins to listen to the interrogator, the offender observes his interest and cooperation and therefore, he will also be more likely to listen. A typical third person theme in this situation might be as follows:

"Mr. Mullen, our investigation clearly indicates that Carm did steal jewelry from the home on Walter Lane. But before you leave I want to talk to both of you today to see if we can get this situation cleared up. The mere fact that both of you are here today shows a great deal of concern as well as cooperation. For that reason, I think we can get this matter resolved. As both of you know, there are good people who simply make a mistake or two in life and there are really bad people who have a history of doing really bad things. I think in this situation a basically good person made an isolated mistake in judgment.

"Let me explain what I'm trying to say. Very recently a man broke into a house with the intent to take a few things. However, while in the house he heard a noise coming from the bedroom. Instead of leaving, this guy went upstairs to see what caused the noise. As he entered the bedroom, he found a woman in total fear. Instead of leaving, he approached the woman, struck her in the head, blindfolded her and then brutally raped her. This guy didn't have to do that. He could have left. Did he? No. He went way beyond simply taking a few things and did something horrible to a very nice person. I think it's obvious this was a bad person with absolutely no morals who took advantage of a situation.

"What he did was just plain wrong. Had he simply taken some property and left, the situation would have been entirely different. It is for this reason that I'm talking to you. If your intent was to just take a few things, not to commit the act of rape, then we need to get this situation resolved. On the other hand, if your intent was to go there with the idea in mind of looking for somebody to rape, or for that matter, if you are the rapist that broke into this other house, then I could understand not wanting to tell the truth. But, if your intent was only to take a few things and not hurt anyone, we need to get this resolved. Also Carm, if this was an isolated incident, that also needs to be explained.

"By not telling your side of the story now, no one will want to believe you later. The time to tell the truth and show your cooperation is now, not later. The most important questions come down to these, were you going to rape the family living in the Walter Lane house? Or, did you just want to take a few things? Furthermore, I'm guessing that you haven't done something like this dozens of times before, have you? I don't think you would have raped any family members if you had come across them, would you? I think you are a basically good guy that did something with the intent of making a few bucks, not wanting to hurt anyone. Am I right? You weren't going to hurt anyone, were you Carm?"

Scenario 3

Jane is accused of shoplifting a $500 designer purse. Jane is in her thirties, has two young children and is married to a doctor. Jane admits taking the purse from the store, but insists that it belongs to her. She ultimately agrees to pay for the purse but denies shoplifting it. Her husband Charles was notified and only agreed to his wife being questioned/interrogated if he was allowed to be present. She has been extremely indignant with store security.

It has been decided to interrogate Jane developing third person themes due to her aggressive denials and her husband's presence. It is believed that developing third person themes, telling her why others have engaged in similar but more serious behavior will be less likely to fuel her aggressive behavior. Also, Jane's embarrassment with her husband's presence must be addressed. This will be accomplished by suggesting to Jane and her husband that her behavior is not unique, that many equally responsible adults have engaged in similar behavior. It will also be suggested that other adults have shoplifted as the result of two primary reasons: an addiction to shoplifting (more socially acceptable) or with the intent to steal and subsequently sell the items to obtain money for drugs or gambling (a more socially unacceptable reason).

Third person theme development will accomplish three goals. First, the socially acceptable theme (addiction) will lessen Jane's embarrassment. Second, these stories will suggest to Jane's husband that her behavior is not that unique. Third, by telling Jane why other people have engaged in similar behavior does not directly accuse her. This will serve to lessen Jane's aggressive behavior.

"Jane, our investigation indicates that you took that purse from the store without paying for it. Charles, our experience suggests that there are basically two types of people that engage in this type of behavior. Let me explain. Charles, not too long ago our surveillance revealed a women about Jane's age taking several designer belts. She was a very nice stay-at-home mom and her husband was a school administrator. She certainly could have paid for the belts. If she and her husband were not making a decent living, then I'd have to assume that she was doing this to supplement her income. But I didn't think that was the case with her. Why did she do this?

"I was perplexed as to why such a nice person did what she did. It wasn't until talking to her that she told me why she believed she took the belts. She said that one day while shopping with her young children, her four-year-old daughter was playing with one of the store toys. When she got home, she realized her child still had the toy and that she did not pay for it. The store never noticed the toy and never charged her. Her intent was not to steal the toy. In fact, had the store brought it to her attention, she would have gladly paid for the item. However, this very innocent incident caused a dramatic turn to occur in her life.

"The next time she went shopping with her daughter, for some unknown reason she gave her daughter a more expensive item to hold while paying for her items. Again, the store didn't mention the item that her child had. She certainly could afford to pay for the item. She told me that in hindsight she thought she did this out of boredom and the need for a little excitement. This behavior however, escalated to her personally taking items from the store. She simply believed that she needed a little more excitement but didn't realize that she had unintentionally developed an addictive behavior. Her addiction was no different than smoking, alcohol, gambling or working to excess. Charles, I'm sure that in your profession you know people that have certain addictions. That does not make a person bad but rather it suggests that that individual needs help.

"Jane, we are only human and we all make mistakes or do things that we would normally never do. I think that you are very similar to this other woman. I don't think that she took the belts to sell them to buy drugs and I don't think that you took the purse to sell it to buy drugs. I think this was the end result of a series of unfortunate incidents that have occurred in your life just like this other woman.

"Charles, Jane is not the typical person that we deal with. In fact, I don't even think that she fully understands why she took the purse. It is obvious that you are a very supportive person and most definitely have Jane's best interest in mind. It is for this reason that we need to resolve this matter. Jane, I don't think that you came into our store to take the purse. I think that for some unexplained reason you simply couldn't help yourself and took the purse. Just like the other woman I was mentioning to you, Jane, you didn't plan on taking the purse, did you?"

Trespassing Themes

1. Minimize the moral seriousness of the trespassing by contrasting the suspect's intent between someone who is just being inquisitive, admiring the property, etc., versus someone who gained access to the property with the idea in mind of committing a burglary, vandalism, arson or engaging in terrorist activity
2. Minimize the perceived seriousness by contrasting the fact that the perpetrator just defaced some of the property versus burning everything down
3. Contrast just looking through the garbage for valuable discards versus doing it with the idea of finding enough personal information to perpetrate identity theft
4. Contrast using force to gain entry versus not using any force
5. Contrast trespassing with weapons or burglary tools in the suspect's possession versus not having any of those items
6. Blame the suspect's unemployment and therefore inability to provide proper housing
7. Blame the influence of alcohol or drugs for causing the suspect to make a wrong decision
8. Blame peer pressure; someone talked the suspect into doing it; someone challenged or dared the suspect to gain access
9. Blame the victim for not having enough warning (no trespassing) signs or for not having the signs in a clearly visible location

10. Blame the suspect for believing that since public property is municipal there are relaxed restrictions for accessing the property

11. Suggest that the suspect believed the "no trespass" signs were not official

12. Suggest that the suspect is not a violent criminal

13. Suggest that the suspect did not have enough time to find a proper entrance to the property

14. Suggest that the suspect believed that it was no big deal

15. Suggest that the suspect was just "hanging out in a cool place," i.e., armory, railroad yard, nuclear site, etc.

16. Suggest that the suspect wanted to see if anything interesting was on the property

17. Suggest that the suspect was challenged by the security or, on the other hand, blame the lack of good security for providing an "open invitation"

18. Suggest that the suspect was simply looking for a place where he would not be bothered

19. Suggest that others are trespassing and the suspect was simply doing what everyone else was doing

20. Suggest that the suspect was using the building or home as a safe place to sleep or stay out of the elements versus trying to steal things or commit some other kind of crime

Theme example: Alex sneaks into a restricted area of the local gas utility company. It appears that someone has been living inside a storage shed on the property. Alex denies being on the property, as well as living in the storage shed.

"Alex, you were observed in the restricted area of the gas company. Our concern is whether or not you were just staying in the shed as a temporary place to live or whether you were doing something very serious in there like molesting children. Fingerprints have been taken from the shed and are being analyzed as are all of our surveillance videos.

"Another concern that we have is that there are homes nearby and an explosion to this site would cause chaos and damage beyond belief. If this wasn't a gas utility we wouldn't have the same concern. For all we know, you may have been testing security at the site with the intention of planning some wide-scale terrorist acts at either this or another gas utility facility. I really don't think that's the case, but who knows? These are the reasons why we're talking to you. You're the only person that knows the true explanation of why you were on this restricted property. Alex, were your intentions to cause damage to the facility or were you simply looking for a place to sleep?"

Utility Theft Themes

These themes focus on the offender's theft of gas, electric or water and can also be modified for cable theft investigations.

A. Blame the victim/company for:

1. High prices
2. Failure to provide a monthly budget plan
3. Not correcting past bills
4. Not repairing problems in a timely manner
5. Not returning repeated phone calls
6. Not providing satisfactory service
7. Unsightly repair or installation
8. Poor anti-theft measures
9. Employees showing or telling suspect how to steal
10. Employees soliciting bribes to facilitate theft

B. Suggest the suspect's intent was to:

1. Save money
2. Provide for his family
3. "Borrow" service for a short time
4. Help others by showing them how to do this
5. Stop when the economic situation improved – not abuse the amount of theft
6. Impress others
7. See if it could be done – the challenge of it
8. Seek revenge, i.e., being overcharged or receiving poor service
9. Help minimize expenses during a financially difficult and stressful time

C. Minimize the suspect's behavior by:

1. Blaming neighbors, co-workers, or family for suggesting the idea
2. Blaming the Internet or underground publications for showing the public how to perpetrate such a theft from the utility/cable company
3. Suggesting anyone would do this if the need and opportunity were present
4. Suggesting that it was an isolated incident versus pattern of behavior
5. Suggesting that the victim (company) could afford the loss
6. Suggesting that the dollar loss was minimal
7. Blaming the company for making it so easy to do – no security measures
8. Contrasting a person who commits a theft from just one utility company with a person who is stealing from all of his utilities suppliers

9. Contrasting utility theft versus a more serious theft such as burglary, robbery, con game, etc.

Theme example: Mr. Smith reports to the electric company that he saw his neighbor Rick bypassing his electric meter with the intent to steal electricity. Rick discovers an investigation is pending and removes the bypass. Rick's electric bill for the last six months has been ninety percent less than normal.

"Rick, we know you've been bypassing your electric meter; we examined it and have determined that it has been tampered with. I can understand why a guy like you would want to bypass the meter. You appear to be a hard-working guy living with his family in a very nice, modest house. Had you been living in a mansion doing something like this, it would mean you were doing this simply out of greed. I'm guessing it was done for just the opposite reason, need. We know that your bills have been way below average for the last six months. We only went back one year reviewing your electric bill charges. It appears that you've lived in your home for eight years. At this point, we don't know if you've been doing this for just the past six months or for the entire eight years.

"It's not like you're stealing your neighbor's electricity or worse yet, putting a gun to someone's head. You've taken electricity from a utility company, which is not the same as taking something from your neighbor. I'm sure this will not break the electric company. But our concern is why you did this and how long you did this. Was this done to better provide for your family? It's obvious that this is something the normal person would not know how to do. This takes someone with some special knowledge about electricity. Therefore, of paramount importance to us is whether you have only done this for yourself or if you have been paid by other people to bypass their electric meters as well. Rick, let's get this resolved, have you been doing this for other people or has this been done only for yourself over these last eight months? Have you done this for other people?"

Vandalism Themes

We see vandalism from all age groups, from kids "tagging" (graffiti) a school building to White House staff allegedly removing the letter "W" from computer keyboards after George W. Bush was elected President. In most instances, no one is physically hurt. Therefore, themes can easily be developed in that most of these crimes are the result of a prank, political statement, intended identification or even beautification.

Suggest to the suspect that his behavior was:

1. Just a prank or joke
2. Part of a gang initiation
3. Done to identify a gang area
4. Done to make the area more attractive ("art" replacing ugliness); to point out the ugliness of something

Minimize the suspect's behavior by pointing out or suggesting that:

1. No one was hurt
2. It was someone else's idea (peer pressure)
3. It was only done to make a political statement
4. It was done as a joke
5. The suspect's intent was to demonstrate his disagreement with posted advertisements, i.e., abortion, anti-smoking, political, etc.
6. This was done because the suspect could not afford to pay for advertisement
7. The community is at fault for not having any programs to keep everyone occupied preventing boredom
8. The victim mistreated the suspect on a prior occasion

9. The area had poor security
10. Alcohol or drugs clouded the suspect's judgment
11. The suspect's young age contributed to the poor decision
12. There is a difference between doing something like this on one occasion versus doing it all of the time
13. This is a situation involving correctable vandalism (new paint) versus a situation that involved permanent damage
14. The suspect was only trying to display his talent

Theme example: Nick has been spray-painting his gang symbols as well as other impressive scenes on local buildings.

"Nick, we know that you have been spray-painting buildings and other structures in the neighborhood. Your work is so easily identifiable from the other graffiti; it's almost like your fingerprint. In fact, it's the most impressive work that I've seen. The reason I can say that is because I've been seeing and investigating this kind of stuff for years. I've got to say that your work, and I use the word work, because that is exactly what it is, is outstanding! It's not just sporadic painting with some identifying gang symbols; it's very well thought out and perfectly designed. It's too bad that you didn't have some way to channel your talent into something more positive, like becoming an artist or marketing designer. I think you have great talent, Nick. However, the community is getting upset at the cost of having to repair your work. I'd like to reach an agreement with you today that you'll stop tagging the locals' property. If we can reach that agreement, then I think we've made progress.

"I don't want to understate the importance of the situation, Nick, but it's not like you've physically hurt anyone or did anything that can't be corrected. Some people in the neighborhood, however, are getting scared. They're asking themselves, 'Is this going to escalate to something being done to my car or worse yet, something to my family members?'

" I really don't think those are your intentions, but I don't know that for sure. I'm sure you know what I'm talking about. I know that you're proud of your gang and to some extent, are keeping some really bad rival gang people out of the neighborhood by telling them who lives here. However, the situation has gotten out of hand. We need to put the breaks on the graffiti from this point on. Can I have your word that you'll cool it? Your intentions aren't to bring this to the next level and harm a local, are they Nick?"

Welfare Fraud Themes

A. Theft of another person's benefits:

1. Blame the victim's poor controls or lack of security
2. Blame other individuals for encouraging the suspect to commit the act
3. Blame the suspect's poor financial situation for causing him to act out of character
4. Suggest that the dollar amount of the fraud will not adversely impact the victim's ability to provide payment for legitimate claims
5. Suggest that the benefits stolen were used for basic necessities versus lavish lifestyle activities such as gambling, drugs, extravagant vacations, etc.
6. Suggest that the legitimate recipient that died was a relative of the suspect versus stealing benefits from an unknown individual
7. Suggest that the intent was to take benefits only for a short time, but unexpected expenses caused the fraud to continue longer than anticipated
8. Suggest that everybody takes advantage of insurance companies;

this is not a unique incident

9. Minimize the dollar amount of the fraud

10. Contrast this type of fraud with a more serious theft involving physical force, such as an armed robbery or burglary

B. Failure to report a job or income while receiving benefits illegally:

1. Suggest that the suspect's intent for failing to report a job was his belief that he might soon quit

2. Suggest that the suspect did not have enough time to report his new job

3. Suggest that the suspect's low-paying income from the new job was necessary to sustain a basic living standard

4. Suggest that the suspect was justified receiving illegal benefits due to the victim's delay in approving the benefits

5. Blame the victim for making it difficult to report a job

Theme example: Veronica's mother died and she failed to report her death to Social Security. She has been receiving and cashing her mother's $500 monthly benefit checks for the last eighteen months. The only difference in their names is the middle initial. The suspect and her husband have low paying jobs and are raising two young children.

"Veronica, our investigation indicates that you have been keeping your mother's Social Security checks. What I think happened was something that was the result of need and opportunity, not the result of dishonesty. If your first name wasn't the same as your mother's, I don't think that you would have done this. I think this was a situation in which you needed some extra money to raise your children and pay your bills. In fact, I bet your mother was helping you financially. You needed this extra money because you're not making $100,000 a year! I deal with people that earn money like that who have kept their deceased family member's benefits;

that is wrong! I think that you would agree with me that a person like that with no need for the benefit money is just plain dishonest. I don't think you're that type of person. I think that you are basically an honest person trying to work hard and provide a better life for your kids. However, when an honest person's income is stagnant or reduced, sometimes an honest person may do uncharacteristic things.

"I think that your intentions were to cash a few checks but unexpected expenses arose which forced you to continue cashing the checks. Another very important fact, Veronica, is that you have only been doing this for 18 months, not 18 years. The benefit you cashed was only $500 a month, not $5,000 a month. I think this was done as a result of a combination of factors. Had any of these factors not been present, you would have never cashed the checks. I think this situation resulted due to the similarity of your name and your mother's name. I also think that the poor controls of the system, the need to provide properly for your children, the loss of financial help from your mother and the rising costs of food, clothing, and education caused you to do something out of need and not greed. This was not done out of greed. This was the result of need, right?"

Workplace Violence Themes

A. Blame the employer's actions or behavior for:

1. Causing employees to constantly work under crisis conditions
2. Having unclear policies in this area
3. Allowing tensions to escalate
4. Allowing corporate profits to deteriorate, due to mismanagement or illegal management
5. Making illogical corporate decisions – laying off the most dedicated employees; hiring outside individuals at higher pay

grades than more deserving current employees, etc.

6. Upsetting employees by being verbally abusive to them
7. Not establishing proper channels of communication for voicing complaints
8. Constantly demeaning employees
9. Mismanagement of employee benefits; eliminating hospitalization, dental, eyeglass or increasing employee premiums; forcing employees to contribute to company stock which is losing value (thereby contributing to workplace frustration)
10. Not having employee counseling available
11. Treating employees as liabilities, not as assets
12. Increasing the employee's workload
13. Reducing employee hours, eliminating or reducing expected hours, bonuses, commissions, overtime, etc.
14. Never saying anything positive, always being negative
15. Insufficient pay raises
16. Management favoritism/discrimination
17. Management allowing rumors to circulate about pending layoffs, company relocation, bankruptcy, etc.
18. Not rewarding employees for extra work
19. Not having better security, which might have prevented the incident – cameras, metal detectors, coded passes for certain areas, etc.

B. Minimize the suspect's behavior:

1. Suggest that this was a one-time incident versus something that he did on a frequent basis
2. Suggest the suspect acted out of frustration versus being vindictive
3. Suggest that the suspect's initial intent was that he was doing it as a joke

4. Blame prior aggressive training, i.e., military, martial arts, growing up in a rough neighborhood, former gang member, etc.
5. Blame affected judgment from alcohol or drugs
6. Blame peer pressure
7. Suggest that the suspect's intent was to stop an undesirable behavior, not to seriously injure anyone
8. Contrast verbal versus physical abuse
9. Contrast having a weapon versus not having a weapon
10. Contrast using a weapon versus not using a weapon or simply displaying weapon
11. Contrast causing injuries versus not causing injuries
12. Contrast causing injuries that can be repaired versus causing permanent scarring or disability
13. Contrast a spur-of-the-moment act versus one that was premeditated

C. Suggest that outside factors are partially to blame:

1. A string of bad luck
2. Personal financial problems
3. Health problems
4. Problems with his children or spouse
5. Conflict with neighbors or friends
6. The stressful commute to and from work

Theme example: Luis engages in workplace violence; outside factors as themes are developed.

"Luis, we all have one really bad day at times – perhaps a day in which we oversleep, rush to take a shower and discover there is no hot water. When we back out of the garage, we run over our kid's bike, causing a flat tire. Driving to work, another car cuts us off, causing us to miss our exit.

We arrive to work an hour late only to discover that we forgot to bring our report, which is to be presented in fifteen minutes. What else could go wrong?

"A co-worker senses you're distraught and becomes increasingly antagonistic. This employee is getting a form of sick pleasure out of your misfortune. This employee doesn't know when to shut up and becomes increasingly more caustic. You tell this employee, not once, but several times to please leave you alone. Does he leave you alone? No. He persists in a very sarcastic manner, asking you, 'Having a bad day, Luis, well are you?'

"This reminds me of the movie *Falling Down* with Michael Douglas. He experiences a day in which everything goes wrong for him and he has reached his breaking point. He becomes increasingly aggressive and violent to the point where he not only hurts people but also begins killing them. Why? Simply because he had a bad day. You had a bad day but didn't start killing people. You couldn't take the badgering of your co-worker any longer and in a split-second decision struck him, but fortunately didn't kill him. You never intended to engage in such a terrible act; in fact you are a non-violent person. What happened was the result of a series of very unfortunate circumstances. Our concern is this, did you do this because of a long-standing hatred of the employee or was this just the result of a series of unfortunate circumstances. I think it was the result of a series of unfortunate circumstances, wasn't it Luis?"

~ Notes ~

Chapter 7

Conclusion

"No legacy is so rich as honesty."

William Shakespeare (1564 – 1616)

I sincerely believe that the interrogation themes presented in this book will greatly assist the investigator in obtaining a legally acceptable confession from the deceptive suspect in the most logical and expeditious manner possible. These interrogation themes are designed to obtain the initial admission of guilt from the suspect. The interrogator must then acquire the necessary intent and details of the crime to transform the primary admission into a fully corroborated confession.

In writing this book, it was also my intent to provide a review of the "Reid Technique of Interviewing and Interrogation" for the reader. Additionally, my objective was to develop a vehicle designed to improve the efficiency and proficiency of the reader by providing as wide an array of interrogation themes and dialogues as possible.

Perhaps my greatest reward will be for the reader to develop the same passion that I feel toward this technique. It is very gratifying, as most of you know, to obtain the initial admission of guilt from the suspect and then convert this acknowledgment into a legally acceptable confession. I believe a great many victims feel helpless, particularly when the crime goes unsolved or worse yet, the suspect gets off on a technicality.

Hopefully, the information provided will help minimize or eliminate many such situations from occurring.

During the past thirty plus-years in this profession, whether interrogating or instructing interrogators, I always think of the victim. My motivation is either obtaining confessions or training others on how to obtain confessions for the victim. I am elated in identifying the offender, knowing that, in some way, this is a form of vindication for the victim. There is also great solace knowing that the offender might not victimize others.

To further assist the investigator, a Reid Interrogation Strategy Form is included. The investigator, prior to an interrogation should consider completing this form so as to act as a quick reference should it become necessary during the interrogation. The suspect's Reid Behavior Analysis Interview responses, case facts, evidence and similar case experience may aid the investigator in completing this form prior to the interrogation. The intent is to have the most appropriate interrogation themes and alternatives selected prior to the interrogation.

As this is the first edition of this book, I am sure that despite the diligence of identifying as many crimes and related themes as possible, I may have unintentionally omitted certain crimes and related themes. If that is the case, I sincerely hope that by following the general principles discussed in this book that you will be able to identify and develop themes for those specific crimes not addressed in this book.

I view this book as a continual work in progress. As technology, new industries and opportunities develop, new types of crimes will also emerge. Therefore, if there are certain crimes that you would like to see addressed in subsequent printings, please e-mail me directly at Lsenese@reid.com or at Lousthemes@aol.com.

Anatomy of Interrogation Themes
THE REID TECHNIQUE OF INTERVIEWING AND INTERROGATION

Reid Interrogation Strategy Form

I. General Interrogation Themes
   A. Alcohol or Drugs
   B. Peer Pressure
   C. Stress
   D.

II. Interrogation themes that offer reasons and excuses that will serve to psychologically, not legally, justify the suspect's behavior. These interrogation themes place the blame onto someone or something else other than the suspect as suggested by available information. Primarily, the victim's actions and behavior are blamed.
   A.
   B.
   C.
   D.
   E.
   F.
   G.

III. Interrogation themes that minimize the moral seriousness of the suspect's criminal behavior, generally contrast what the suspect committed to something much worse.
   A.
   B.
   C.
   D.

E

F.

G.

IV. Third Person Themes

    A. Self

    B. Stories from the media

    C. Similar cases

    D.

V. Alternatives

    A. First time versus several

    B. Planned out a long time or just a short time

    C. Sorry versus glad the act was committed

    D. Your idea versus someone else's idea

    E. Spur-of-the-moment versus premeditated

    F.

Copies of this book can be purchased on line
at www.reid.com

Louis C. Senese, Vice President
John E. Reid and Associates, Inc.
209 West Jackson Blvd., 4th Floor
Chicago, IL 60606
1-800-255-5747